"What's she saying? What's he thinking? This book gets in the head and heart of what guys and girls say and think about each other. Heather knows more teens than the captain of the football team. Tom will make you laugh and learn. This is a book teens will read and parents will trust."
—*Leith Anderson, Pastor, Wooddale Church,*
Eden Prairie, Minnesota

"How awesome would it be if you could somehow crawl inside the brain of the opposite sex to figure out what in the world is going on in there? Well now you can (almost)! Each chapter of *That's What She Said, That's What He Said* will give you an up-close look at how the opposite sex thinks, why they act the way they do, and how you can understand and get along with them a little better. I know your parents are probably on your case to read a little more often...so why not start with this book; I think you'll be glad you did!"
—*Kurt Johnston, Pastor to Students, Saddleback Church*

"Who can figure out teenagers? Heather Flies and Tom Richards can! With a witty, wise, engaging back-and-forth style, they take on what it is like to be a teen in today's world. Any teen (or adult who works with teens) will find great insights on gender differences and how those differences matter in everything from the daily schedule and basic conversations to decisions about sex. I'll buy copies for all the teens in our family—and so should you!"
—*Jay Barnes, President, Bethel University*

"This is a great resource that anyone who works with teenagers can use. Tom and Heather do a great job of writing to young teens in a compelling, fun, and ultimately complete way. These books would be a great addition to a relationship retreat, a series on love, sex, and dating, or even the transition from middle school to high school. Any small group leader will find it extremely helpful in bringing up the things young teens need to talk about but often don't know how to. The book not only engages them, but provides practical help."

—*Tic Long, Executive Director, Youth Specialties*

"I can still remember when I crossed the line from 'Girls have cooties...' to 'I like cooties.' All of sudden, everything changed! It was like learning to walk all over again. All of the normal stuff: burping loud, body noises, bad breath, B.O.—it was like overnight I'm realizing, 'Ohmygosh, girls don't like that stuff! And...um...I like girls.' It would have been so much easier if I could have shared this journey with two wise, fun, friendly voices like Heather Flies and Tom Richards—people who clearly understand the struggles, and questions, and weirdness of being a teenager!"

—*Dr. Duffy Robbins, Professor of Youth Ministry, Eastern University*

"Teenage girls, including my own, always want information about boys. But in an age when information is readily available from far too many unreliable sources, it's reassuring to know that someone with integrity, training, insight, and experience is willing to step out and offer views on how girls can better understand and relate to boys in a healthy and appropriate way. Heather is firmly grounded not only in Scripture, but in years of consistently demonstrating Christ's love to teenagers. Everyone who knows her would agree: God gifted her in an extraordinary way. And now she shares her insights in a compelling book that teenage girls will definitely want to read."

—*Mary Pawlenty, wife, mother of girls, and former First Lady of Minnesota*

"that's what **she** said"

"that's what **he** said"

everything teens want to know about the opposite sex— from his and her perspectives

HEATHER FLIES and TOM RICHARDS

summerside
PRESS

Summerside Press™
Minneapolis, MN 55337
www.summersidepress.com

That's What She Said, That's What He Said
Everything Teens Want to Know about the Opposite Sex—
from His and Her Perspectives
© 2011 by Heather Flies and Tom Richards

ISBN 978-160936-220-1

Unless otherwise noted, Scripture is taken from the Holy Bible, New
International Version®, NIV®. Copyright © 1973, 1978, 1984, 2011 by Biblica,
Inc.™ Used by permission of Zondervan. All rights reserved worldwide.

Scripture marked The Holy Bible, New Living Translation (NLT), copyright
1996, 2004, 2007. Used by permission of Tyndale House Publishers, Inc.,
Wheaton, Illinois.

Cover and interior design by Aesthetic Soup | Minneapolis, MN 55379

*Summerside Press is an inspirational publisher offering fresh, irresistible
books to uplift the heart and engage the mind.*

Printed in China.

This book is dedicated to the thousands of teens who shared their lives with us for nearly two decades in youth ministry. That's right, twenty years of fart jokes, Mountain Dew, pizza, sleeping on camp beds, and teenage drama...and we've lived to tell about it! Some kids made us laugh 'til it hurt, and others made us cry...but mostly laugh. They have all taught us a thing or two about how and why God made guys and girls wonderfully unique.

Your fingerprints are all over our lives, and we are so grateful!

"It is important to

understand some

of the...ways men

and women are unique

if we hope to live

together in harmony."

DR. JAMES DOBSON

Contents

Foreword ix

Introduction 1

Section One

What Girls/Guys Should Know 5

Chapter 1: My Time, Your Time, Our Time 9

Chapter 2: There's Nothing Like a Hero 15

Chapter 3: I Am Not a Mind Reader 21

Chapter 4: How Do I Look? 27

Chapter 5: God's Not Finished with Me Yet 33

Section Two

What Girls/Guys Aren't Thinking About 39

Chapter 6: I Am Who I Am 43

Chapter 7: What the Future Holds 49

Chapter 8: How I Get Attention 55

Chapter 9: Long-Term Purity 61

Section Three

What Girls/Guys Won't Tell You 67

Chapter 10: The Meaning of Words 71

Chapter 11: It's All About Me 77

Chapter 12: What You Think Matters 83

Chapter 13: No Baggage Needed 89

Chapter 14: He Loves Me, He Loves Me Not 95

Section Four

What Gets Girls/Guys Worked Up 101

Chapter 15: I Need a Little R-E-S-P-E-C-T 105

Chapter 16: Do You See What I See? 111

Chapter 17: Your Power Over Me .117

Chapter 18: Thinking of You 123

Chapter 19: I Want to Be Close to You 129

Section Five

What Girls/Guys Think About Sex .135

Chapter 20: You Thinking What I'm Thinking? 139

Chapter 21: An Appetite for Sex 145

Chapter 22: What Are You Saying? 151

Chapter 23: Setting Boundaries 157

Chapter 24: Moving the Boundaries 163

Chapter 25: What the Future Holds 169

My Commitment Statements 174

Books by Heather and Tom 178

About the Authors 170

That's What She Said, That's What He Said,

is a must-read for every student who desires to know and honor God with every relationship and friendship. As a youth pastor for over thirty years, I have spent endless hours in the trenches of teenage relationships. I believe this book is a powerful tool providing valuable perspective on relational insights. The innovative format utilized in this book is based on honest reflection from each gender's perspective about what the other is truly thinking and feeling. This work is invaluable for youth ministry professionals, volunteers in student ministry, parents of teens, and most importantly, students themselves!

I can't think of two more gifted and qualified youth ministry professionals than Tom Richards and Heather Flies. I have known Tom and Heather since their early days in youth ministry and have watched them become beloved youth communicators. Tom and Heather both embody the highest levels of integrity and commitment to students. Their lives are committed to the process of discipling students. Their life calling is to provide an increasingly passionate environment for students to know God.

Tom's keen insight, unique discernment, and relational style of ministry stems from vast amounts of time spent with students. Tom's passion for seeing students on fire for God provides a wonderfully rich platform and ability to communicate honestly without holding back on sensitive issues. Heather has an infectious love, robust passion, and unending devotion to student ministry. If you have ever been fortunate enough to be embraced by Heather, then you know of her total "all in" approach to life and ministry! They both possess a God-given ability to communicate to the heart of teenage students.

Tom and Heather have accurately, yet playfully, captured the vast differences between the genders. These pages provide a plethora of wisdom based on God's Word. You will find this penetrating and reflective style of comparing perspectives both timely and refreshing. The chapters will have you laughing and crying as you quickly relate to the timeless stories. These major topics are on the minds of every American teenager, and this engaging format provides an avenue into their hearts. Sit back, grab your favorite caffeinated beverage, and jump into *That's what She Said, That's What He Said*.

—*Tim Block, Pastor to Youth and Families, Mission Viejo, CA.*

introduction

Guys, have you ever noticed that girls go to the bathroom together in packs? And once they're in there, what they talk about is a mystery to the rest of us. Have you ever asked a buddy, "Is your girlfriend this emotional too?" Do you wonder what a girl's idea of the perfect guy is?

Girls, have you ever noticed that guys always seem to be scratching themselves? What's worse is that they don't seem to be embarrassed to scratch in public! Are you confused when they treat you one way when you're alone and another way when they're with their friends? And what's with the need to turn everything into a competition?

You're not alone. Since the beginning of time, guys and girls have struggled to make sense of the opposite gender. It's almost like we're from different planets—or, at the very least, speak different languages. What if you had access to a translator? Someone to interpret the foreign ways so that they made sense to you? A cheat sheet, if you will.

Insider insight might help you find answers to situations that have confused you for years. You could remove a significant amount of stress from your social life. Healthy opposite gender friendships and dating relationships could be a reality. You might even become president of the United States of America! Okay, maybe that's taking it a bit too far, but you get the idea. This could be huge!

Here is that cheat sheet!

We once heard guys and girls compared to waffles and spaghetti (*Men Are Like Waffles—Women Are Like Spaghetti* by Bill and Pam Farrel). As weird as it sounds, we think it fits.

Guys, you're like a waffle. Your life is filled with a bunch of different compartments, little squares. When the syrup is poured on the waffle, it goes into the separate squares and stays there. Life is like that for you. When you're at football, you're at football. You're not thinking about homework, your dog's flea issue, or your girlfriend. You're thinking about what route the receiver is running and how hard you're going to hit him. You're like a waffle.

Girls, you're more like spaghetti. A bowl of spaghetti is all intertwined. One noodle is wrapped around and through nine other noodles and the sauce is covering everything. Life is like that for you. If you are at drama rehearsal, you want to be all there, but other drama is vying for your attention. Your best friend is mad at you because you agreed to go with another group of girlfriends to the dance. You gained two pounds last week. Your dad told you if you don't bring your math grade up, you won't be getting your license on your birthday. How can you be expected to focus on your lines with all that on your mind? You're like spaghetti.

In the pages to follow, we poke fun at guys and girls and reveal the differences that make you uniquely special. It's our hope that you'll laugh at yourself when you think, *That's so me!* and respond to the challenges at the end of each chapter with a certain humility. We want to point out that our insight into guys and girls is in general terms, so don't be worried if you don't fit the standard mold (there is no such thing!).

In fact, you'd be hard pressed to find two people more different from the stereotypes we portray in this book than its authors. Heather is wired like a lot of guys—she loves monster truck shows and can spit with the best of 'em. She can beat most college football players in arm wrestling and gives spine-crushing hugs to everyone in her path. She's a force to be reckoned with! Tom, on the other hand, talks as much as most girls. He tells stories and cries in movies. His clothes are of better quality and fashion than the women in his life. He also drinks Diet Coke, but only through a straw and never out of the can.

But we know guys and girls. Between the two of us, we've logged thirty-three years working with teenagers. We've seen, heard, and experienced a lot of hormones, drama, and differences. Our goal in writing this book was to give you an honest look at yourself, and the other gender as well. Tom, having mentored and ministered to guys, will be giving girls an inside look at the ways of a guy. Heather, knowing and loving the female gender, will part the clouds of confusion for the guys. You may be tempted to use this information to manipulate the opposite sex—but we trust you're bigger and better than that! If used correctly, these insights will help you build godly relationships and understand and appreciate the opposite gender. It's our hope that after some fun, yet deep reading, each of you will feel better about who God created you to be AND celebrate the differences God created in guys and girls. It's all good!

–Heather and Tom

The Holy Spirit helps us in our
weakness. For example, we
don't know what God wants us
to pray for. But the Holy Spirit
prays for us with groanings that
cannot be expressed in words.

ROMANS 8:26 NLT

**Anybody who knows everything
should be told a thing or two.**

FRANKLIN P. JONES

4

SECTION 1

what girls/guys should know

There are a lot of things girls think they know about guys and that guys think they know about girls. But much of what we think we know is just incorrect information.

There are truths we should know—truths that will help us all understand each other. Like all guys really want to be a hero. She may not be able to imagine her guy friends as heroes, and he may not be able to imagine himself protecting or saving anyone, but the desire is there.

Here is the real scoop on what girls and guys are thinking. Think about how it feels to be in their shoes for awhile. Understanding their perspective changes how we think, how we react, and how we pray. So here are a few truths you should know about those guys/girls in your life.

Quotes are from teens in response to a Facebook questionnaire about relationships.

"Girls feel most respected by guys when they put down the video game controller and text us back."

"Chivalry is better than how 'cool' you are."

that's what she said

"A girl wants to be captivating, but help us learn how to make you the hero!"

"Girls want to be loved, cherished, and protected; but not so protected that we can't do anything. We are still our own people!"

"We don't always understand, but we try our best and always *want* to understand."

"We love to be adored and be made into the 'Superhero Boyfriend.'"

that's what he said ◄ · · · ·

"It's okay to tell us exactly what's on your mind."

"We feel closer when you don't constantly criticize everything."

Chapter 1

....

my time, your time, our time

....

i'd rather spend all
my time with you.

i'd rather play video
games sometimes.

> ## i'd rather spend all my time with you.

Sometimes I ask girls, "What would be great about being a guy?" Without a doubt, the top two answers are (1) being able to pee standing up, and (2) not having a period. You guys do have it pretty good. Most of you can even roll out of bed ten minutes before you have to leave the house—throw on a pair of jeans (that are lying on the floor from the night before), a T-shirt, a hat—and still look good. Do you appreciate that gift? We envy you!

Just for a moment, take a look into the world of being a girl. Even though each girl is unique, most girls want similar things.

The average girl's best day:

9:30 a.m.	Wake up surrounded by girls who slept over
9:35 a.m.	Talk about what we think the guys are doing
9:45 a.m.	Text boyfriend to say "Good morning!"
9:47 a.m.	Breakfast of half a bagel and an orange
10:00 a.m.	Workout
11:00 a.m.	Check Facebook and post on my boyfriend's wall
Noon	Shower, choose outfit strategically, and get ready
2:00 p.m.	Meet girlfriends at the mall to shop
3:00 p.m.	Buy matching shirts for the Sadie Hawkin's Dance
5:00 p.m.	Go home to change outfits and get ready to meet him.
7:00 p.m.	Date night! (I hope he notices my new highlights!)
11:00 p.m.	Home after a sweet kiss
Midnight	Fall asleep listening to our song repeating on my iPod

Did you notice how much she thought of her boyfriend throughout her day? And the times listed were only the notable ones—she actually had thoughts of him about 137 more times!

Girls think about guys a lot...and we assume they think about us as much as we think about them. This is what often gets us in trouble. We tend to overwhelm guys with our calls, texts, and requests to get together. And often don't understand why guys aren't doing the same.

One summer, having just returned from an awesome week of Junior High Summer Camp, I had to deal with the effects of this over-

i'd rather play video games sometimes.

Imagine waking up one morning as a guy. Besides the strange smell, hairy legs, and lump in your throat, what else would be different? So much! The way guys are wired is so unlike girls that their idea of a dream schedule might surprise you. Even though each person is unique, most guys wake up with a similar day in mind.

The average guy's best day:

11:30 a.m.	Wake up early
11:45 a.m.	Push-ups and arm curls in front of the mirror
Noon	Eat six eggs, half a pound of bacon, and four donuts to jumpstart the metabolism
12:30 p.m.	Break out the new video game
2:30 p.m.	Eat an entire pizza
3:00 p.m.	Nap time (my growing body wears me out)
6:00 p.m.	Get dressed for the day
6:30 p.m.	Someone feed me dinner before I starve to death!
7:00 p.m.	Time with the girlfriend (lots of kissing—if I'm lucky)
8:30 p.m.	Man time with the guys—arm-pit farts, grunting, and scratching
Midnight	Mountain Dew sugar coma kicks in—fall asleep in front of TV

Did you notice that this guy didn't think much about girls during the day? And when he did, he was a lot more interested in kissing one than gazing into her eyes and sharing his feelings.

If you believe guys think about girls as much as girls think about them, you may need to adjust your expectations. It's often those expectations that overwhelm guys.

Jake was Jessica's first serious boyfriend. It was their freshman year in high school, and they were at different schools. Those butterflies in Jake's stomach flew away after a couple of weeks as Jessica demanded more and more of his time on the phone. It started in the morning even before he woke up—text messages pouring in one after the other. And if he didn't respond within a few minutes, she'd send a

i'd rather spend all my time with you.
continued

abundance. My first day back in the office, I got a call from the mom of a guy who was at camp with us. She said, "Heather, I just don't know what to do! Since Matt has been back from camp, a girl has called our house eleven times! Matt talked to her once, but won't answer the phone anymore. Is this normal for her to call like this?"

Unfortunately, I had to tell the mom that although the eleven calls were excessive, this was normal behavior for a young teenage girl. They get excited when they like a guy, and their reason doesn't always override the desire to talk with him and spend time with him.

If you have a girl in your life who is overwhelming you with contact and attention, you have permission to say (as kindly as you can), "I really do like you, but I need to have time with my family, homework, and guy friends too." She might be slightly hurt at first, but you need to help her draw a healthy boundary. It is something that can be worked through. She needs the same time away from you as you need from her. Understand that her frequent calls and texts are her way of letting you know she is thinking about you. Then, make a genuine effort to call or text her more than you naturally would. An "I'm thinking of you" text in the middle of the day can go a long way!

> **Girls send and receive about eighty text messages a day, while guys send and receive only thirty.**
> From a Pew survey of 800 guys and girls ages 12–17.

Try this in the next week:

1. If a girl is overwhelming you with her contact, kindly let her know you need less. It's a tough conversation, but if it doesn't happen, you'll become bitter.
2. After responding to a couple texts, set a time to talk later in the day and shut off your phone to be with the guys.
3. When you do think about her, let her know.

i'd rather play video games sometimes.
continued

text to ask if he was mad at her. So much for sleeping in!

Jake and Jessica talked on the phone every day. When every day turned into every few hours, Jake became frustrated. And when every few hours turned into constant texting between calls, he was at the end of his rope. At the same time, Jessica was constantly disappointed and was feeling like Jake was brushing her off. Their relationship crumbled.

Sometimes teenage guys (even adult men) would rather play video games than talk on the phone. In fact, they'd rather do a hundred things—even awful things like get a root canal or work on algebra—than have a phone glued to their ear. As part of their natural development they're still in a stage of thinking about themselves much more than thinking about what girls are doing.

Don't take it personally if a guy you are interested in doesn't seem as excited to talk as you are. In the same way, you're probably not as excited about his dream schedule at the top of this chapter. That's because guys and girls are wired differently, even down to how we enjoy spending our time—especially when it comes to communicating.

> Percent of households with a device used *primarily* for gaming: 73%.

Try this in the next week:

1. Save your next gabfest for a girlfriend. God gave you girlfriends for a reason!
2. Wait for a guy to pursue you. It may sound old-fashioned, but it will mean more to him if he initiates a call or date...and it will mean more to you too.
3. Contact him less and let him know how much you enjoy hearing from him.
4. Ask him if you can spend time together playing video games.

Chapter 2

there's nothing like a hero

> i want to feel safe and protected.

> i want to be a hero.

i want to feel safe and protected.

When I was little, I used to fake being asleep at the end of a long car ride just so my dad would have to carry me into the house and tuck me into bed. I remember, even at age five, feeling so protected and safe in his arms. Every time he was behind the wheel, I felt secure. When I knew he was home, I slept fearlessly. I had full confidence in him.

The girls I talk with communicate a similar experience or hope in regard to their fathers. Girls have an inborn, natural desire to be protected by a man. As a girl gets older, that job of protection transfers from her father to the young man her heart chooses—guys just like you. No pressure, right?

> The website safetygirl.com offers personal pepper spray that comes in fashionable lipstick-looking containers for only $6.99!

This desire to be protected doesn't mean a girl can't fend for herself. Many girls can. They are intelligent, strong, independent, and some even excel in self-defense classes! Wanting to feel safe is a desire, not necessarily a need. Isn't it cool that, as a guy, you can help to fulfill that desire?

Many guys like the idea of having a girlfriend or friend that is a girl—someone to make him feel good about himself, someone to come and watch him dominate the court, someone to move him up the social ladder. But the truth is most teenage guys don't get the importance of the role they play as boyfriend or guy friend.

You are capable and up for the challenge! Being a protector could look like this for you:

- When you take a girl out on a date (a driving date), you are careful about how you drive. You are responsible for her safety. You set aside your need for speed and drive responsibly.
- You consider her reputation. You are no longer thinking just about you. You ask yourself these kinds of questions: Will her reputation be challenged because of the party, movie, or place I choose to go to? Does being with me enhance her good reputation?

i want to be a hero.

Marcus is shiny—by that I mean he is all smiles all the time. When God passed out optimism and positive thinking, he spilled extra on Marcus. His character is uncompromising, and he loves God. Most moms and dads would line up around the block to get a guy like Marcus to date their daughter.

Marcus is also all boy. He eats like a horse. He gets a kick out of the noises his body makes—and he can make most of those noises happen on command. He's athletic, competitive, and strong. No matter what he eats, it seems to turn to muscle. (The same cookie dough that would make most people fat works like an anti-fat, muscle-building supplement on him—life isn't fair!)

You'd probably never guess that Marcus's secret ambition in life is to beat up a bad guy in order to defend a girl. Not just punch him in the face or knock him down—Marcus wants to annihilate the bad guy. He longs for the perfect opportunity to pummel another guy for a good reason. Marcus wants to be a hero.

Most guys want to be heroes. It's part of how they're wired. Guys' bodies make about ten times more testosterone than girls'. Testosterone is a hormone that affects risk-taking decisions, sexual appetites, and body development. It's because of testosterone that guys are usually bigger, stronger, and hairier than girls. It helps with being tough too, and guys try really hard to be tough.

Sometimes guys want to impress their friends so badly, they make costly mistakes in their effort to be a hero. At their worst, guys:

- use girls as sexual pawns
- joke and brag about physical experiences
- bully weaker guys
- win at all cost in sports
- cheat or lie to maintain an image

> Spider-Man is said to be the all-time most popular superhero because he spans four eras—the '60s, '70s, '80s, and 2000s.

i want to feel safe and protected.
continued

- As you hang out with your guy friends, you make sure they treat her with respect—in how they look at her and talk to or about her.
- If her parents have set guidelines—curfew, not being in the house alone, limited texts or calls, etc.—you honor and follow those rules. You remember her protection is being transferred to you. Prove yourself worthy of that incredible responsibility!
- If you are dating, you, as a couple, determine godly, sexual boundaries, and you do not pressure her to go beyond those boundaries.

This may be a new concept for many guys, but it's the reality of guy/girl relationships. Girls have a natural desire to look to guys for protection. As you experience the benefits of being a worthy protector, you will want to make the girls in your life feel even safer in your presence, and that's one of the things God created you to do. You have a natural desire to protect and respect girls. You want to be their hero. Do it well!

. . . .

Try this in the next week:
1. Make a list of the ways you could protect the women and girls in your life right now.
2. Brainstorm with some other guys you know about what God has given specifically to guys that allows them to be good protectors.
3. Start protecting your girl friends by confronting guys who talk poorly or sexually about girls, and refuse to engage in those kinds of conversations yourself.

i want to be a hero. continued

• refuse help (this is why guys won't ask for directions)

Being a hero looks a little like old-fashioned chivalry. Every guy has potential for chivalry, and you should expect to see traces of it in guy friends. It may be something small like opening a door for you. Or it may take form in his desire to protect you. The story of Marcus offers a little insight into the mind of a guy, as well as an example of what extent guys will go to protect girls. They can do that by driving carefully, choosing good entertainment on dates, respecting boundaries, and honoring girls even in the midst of locker room talk (the list could go on and on). Guys need help figuring out that being a hero is more than brawn and bravado—its real consideration, protection, and respect. And girls need a little help in letting them feel like heroes by not belittling their efforts and thanking them for their heroic gestures—no matter how small.

While girls want to be rescued princesses, guys are wired to be heroes. And just like a Disney story, that can be an awesome combination.

. . . .

Try this in the next week:

1. Acknowledge the next time a guy treats you right. It will spur him on to *keep* treating you well because he wants to be a hero in your eyes.
2. If you have a brother or close guy friend, share with him your ideas of what it means to be a hero. Something you say might stick!

Chapter 3

i am not a mind reader

> i want you to read my mind.

> i don't know why you're upset—just tell me.

i want you to read my mind.

A movie came out in the late 1990s about a guy who had the power to read the minds of women. Every thought they had, he could hear as clearly as if the women were speaking right to him. After the initial shock (can you imagine hearing EVERY girl's thoughts as you walk down the hallway between classes!?), he started to use the power to his advantage. As he responded to their unspoken desires, they fell into the palm of his hand! If a woman thought, *I wish he'd notice my new haircut*, he would look at her lovingly and say, "Your hair looks incredible! I love it!" She would melt. He was every girl's dream!

Girls, for some crazy reason, want guys to read their minds and respond accordingly. Maybe it's some kind of sick game we enjoy playing or maybe we've simply watched too many chick flicks, but it's definitely a reality guys face when they hang out with girls. You've probably experienced a girl being mad at you for seemingly no reason, and you were wondering, *What did I do?* More than likely, it's not what you did, but what you didn't do. She had an idea in her mind of how she wanted you to behave, and you failed to live up to that idea.

> Many of the unrealistic expectations girls embrace come from watching romantic movies.

Stinks, doesn't it? How can you meet an expectation that isn't even communicated? Sadly, you're not the only victim. Girls have the same unspoken expectations for their friends, parents, teachers, and coaches. This trend is the major contributor to the drama that's in her life. She expects one thing. Reality delivers something else. Drama rises.

Guys truly can't fathom all that runs through a girl's mind when she is with them. Sharing a typical teenage girl's train of thought as she sits next to a guy in a movie theater might help. It would sound something like this:

> *I'm so glad he's sitting next to me.... I totally know he did it on purpose.... I wonder if he likes my perfume? I wish*

> # i don't know why you're upset— just tell me.

Picture this scene: Paul and Tim—best friends—have a conflict. Paul sees Tim check out his girlfriend with his wandering eyes. Paul is upset and confused about how to handle the situation. He comes up with three possible solutions:

1. Ignore Tim. He can shop as long as he doesn't buy.
2. Punch Tim. No words needed. Conflict solved.
3. Verbally assault Tim. Distract him from the situation by teasing him, threatening him, or putting him in his place.

Guys don't necessarily work through all of their feelings to come to a solution. They're not necessarily aware of all of their feelings because they don't commit a lot of time to analyzing relationships and conversations. They're wired differently than girls.

If a guy were a machine, the machine would have one switch, labeled "on/off." If a girl were a machine, it would need a room full of panels filled with dials, blinking lights, knobs, and switches—and would require an instruction manual more complicated than anything that's been developed for NASA's Mission Control Center! Most girls are that much more complicated than guys.

When a guy likes a girl, he desperately wants to please her. He wants her to admire him and respect him. He wants her to be happy.

But so much of the time, girls aren't happy because they create unrealistic expectations for guys—expectations that are not clear. And unmet expectations leave girls frustrated over and over again.

You might want to spend time alone with a guy, but at the last minute he invites other friends along too. You might want him to bring you chocolates on Valentine's Day, but instead he brings red and pink Starbursts. You might want him to open the door for you, but it comes

> Mirror neurons (in our brains) suggest that we pretend to be in another person's mental shoes, according to a neuroscientist at the UCLA School of Medicine.

i want you to read my mind.

he would hold my hand—wait! I think he moved his hand closer to mine! Does he want to hold my hand?... I wonder how many kids he wants someday. I want four.... I bet he wants four too...he would be such a great dad....

The movie ends. The typical guy gets up, walks out, farting along the way—hoping no one notices. He's been holding that gas in the whole movie! It was the only thing he could think about!

Are you picking up on the differences? So, what do you do with this information? Well to start, simply acknowledge that there is a lot more going on in a girl's head (and heart) than in yours. Don't let a girl's drama and romantic expectations put you on an emotional roller coaster. Let her know you want to please her, but you need to know how to do that. Ask her often what she is thinking or if you can do anything for her. Let her know she needs to tell you what she's thinking—you can't read her mind!

. . . .

Try this in the next week:

1. Ask a female friend about her expectations of guys, and keep those in mind the next time you aren't sure how to respond to a girl.
2. Pray that God would give you sensitivity to the girls in your life.
3. If you are going out with a girl, say something like, "What are two things I'm not doing in our relationship that I could start doing?"
4. If a girl does get upset with you, try not to take it personally. Girls' expectations and internal drama alone are enough to upset them.

i don't know why you're upset— just tell me. continued

crashing in your face while he strides ahead. You might want him to call you every day but he only calls twice a week. On a weekly or even daily basis girls get upset when guys don't meet their expectations. And it's even more maddening for the guys when they don't know why you're upset.

How many times have you given a guy the silent treatment because you've been angry? Or maybe you've been cold or distant when you've been with him. And after all that, he doesn't even notice? Chances are, he may have noticed, but had no idea what to do. If you look back at the three solutions above, there are two he will never want to use on you ("verbal assault" and "punching"). That only leaves him with "ignore it."

You might try this next time you're faced with frustration or anger: level with the guy. Be direct and clear. Let him know exactly why you're upset. Remember, he wants to please you. He wants to make it right. But he is not a mind reader and he doesn't have anywhere near the number of switches, dials, and controls that you have. Give him a little direction.

· ·

Try this in the next week:

1. If a guy disappoints you or frustrates you, level with him. Pray for the right words. Be direct. And keep the conversation short.
2. The Bible tells us to be quick to listen and slow to speak. Look for an opportunity to extend grace and patience to a guy. Sometimes it's better to give someone the benefit of the doubt than to address every hurt feeling or concern.

Chapter 4

how do
i look?

i struggle with
comparing myself
to other girls.

i don't notice new
hairdos, shoes,
or nail polish.

i struggle with comparing myself to other girls.

Because of insecurity, girls often get caught up in comparing themselves to other girls. Guys do it sometimes too—especially on the field, court, in the weight room, or classroom. But for girls, it's almost constant. At school. At church. At the mall. Even in their own homes. How can that be? There are many reasons.

Boyfriends. In their self-centered perspective, it seems like all their friends have boyfriends or at least guys that are interested in them. Even if they aren't super interested in dating or their parents won't let them date, they still feel left out. They watch closely how guys treat other girls. They compare and contrast those actions to how they *perceive* guys are treating them. Sometimes the pressure is so great, they end up going out with guys who don't treat them well or aren't good influences just so they can feel like they measure up in the comparison game.

Fashion. Have you ever taken the time to check out the ridiculous amount of fashion girls have to choose from? If not, you should. Just walk into a Hollister or American Eagle and compare the girls' selections to the guys'. You'll notice a few differences. First, the girls' sections are more expansive. Second, the sizes are incredibly small. Third, the prices are just as expensive as the guys', for a lot less material. No matter the physical size or economic status of a teenage girl, she feels the pressure to wear what all the other girls are wearing.

> Prior to the mid-nineteenth century, most clothing was custom-made, tailored to the body-type and style of the individual woman, as opposed to today's practice of being mass-produced to fit the general public.

Looks. Our culture has made the definition of physical beauty pretty clear. If a girl wants to be considered attractive by others—mainly guys—she feels she needs to have a noticeable chest, skinny waste, toned legs and arms, good complexion, and straight blonde hair. This crazy ideal clashes with the following facts: (1) God created

i don't notice new hairdos, shoes, or nail polish.

I have never noticed a girl's shoes in my entire life. Which leads me to think that if a guy compliments a girl on her shoes, he's most likely just trying to butter her up. Most guys never look that low (they're so enamored by a beautiful face!). This may come as a disappointment to you, especially when you find the perfect pair for the perfect outfit.

Guys generally have two pairs of shoes: tennis shoes and the "other" pair. Tennis shoes usually get the job done. A good pair of tennis shoes work for anything from gym class to church. For very special occasions the other pair is needed. These less necessary and certainly less comfortable shoes are standard for weddings, funerals, and those "dress up" type school dances. They may or may not fit correctly, but who cares when it's only once or twice a year, right?

> Want to see guys gazing intently into a mirror? Just go to the weight room!

While most guys may not care much about shoes, they care about other things, like cars. And some guys think about cars in as much detail as some girls think about shoes. They care about details like rims, turbochargers, and subwoofers.

Where girls care a lot about *appearance*, guys care a lot about *performance*, like:
- How fast they can drive their cars.
- How often they can dunk on a regulation hoop.
- How much money they can make.
- How much weight they can lift.

They may also track ESPN's Sport Center like it's their religion, memorize and recite ridiculous lines from funny movies, or collect the newest cheats on their favorite video games like girls collect shoes. Guys care a lot about details, just different details.

It would mean a lot to a guy for you to go to one of his games (sports or video) and watch him play. That's it! Just be there and stare straight ahead—he'll be all about that.

i struggle with comparing myself to other girls. continued

us all to be different—varying in sizes and hair color; (2) As girls move through their teenage years, their bodies naturally (without any change to diet or exercise!) become more shapely (bigger hips, softer body); (3) Teenagers all have trouble with their complexion. Yet, a girl will compare herself to her best friend, classmate, teammate, or magazine model and do all she can to make herself look like that ideal—even if it means harming herself.

Guys, one of the biggest ways you can help a girl is by being careful of what you say. As girls are caught in this comparison game, they are uber aware and sensitive to the things you say. If you make a side comment about how attractive a certain model, actress, or class-mate is, many girls who hear that comment will take that to mean that is what *she* needs to look like. Also, if you choose to make a negative comment, even jokingly, about a girl's looks, it will make a huge, neg-ative impact on her view of herself. Knowing that most girls seriously and continuously struggle with comparing themselves to others, you can encourage her by remarking on her unique qualities. Your words hold great power—use them well!

. . . .

Try this in the next week:

When you are around girls, be aware of the following:
1. She is paying close attention to what you say about other girls.
2. She is comparing herself to every other girl in the room (and usually losing).
3. Your encouraging words—especially concerning her charac-ter—can build her up in a good, true way.

i don't notice new hairdos, shoes, or nail polish. continued

It must be frustrating for girls to spend hours getting ready for a special night only to have a guy say a quick "you look nice" and then start talking about something altogether different. And it is probably maddening for a girl whose six-inch haircut goes unnoticed all week by her boyfriend. It's not that guys are so self-absorbed that they don't notice the little details about you. It's more like they haven't learned to care about the same things you care about, or to mention them.

Heather is great at noticing haircuts, and she likes to point them out with a compliment when she sees one. But over time she realized that she was annoying one of her guy friends. It sort of bugged him that she was always talking about his hair. What motivated Heather to compliment her friend's haircuts? She probably wants the same attention when she gets her hair cut. But guys just don't think like that.

Don't get me wrong—guys notice girls' physical beauty. But sometimes they're so caught up in noticing the whole package they fail to notice the details that matter so much to you. Don't take it too personally. For now, consider finding the affirmation you crave about your accessories and hair among your girlfriends. Eventually guys will start commenting on the details, but in the meantime, focus on your internal beauty as much as you do on the external.

Try this in the next week:

1. Ask one of your guy friends to tell you about something that interests him. Who knows, maybe you'll learn something interesting.
2. Ask a guy friend if you can tell him about something that interests you. He might learn something interesting too!

Chapter 5

God's not finished with me yet

i may try to fix you.

my brain is a few years behind my body.

i may try to fix you.

When I was in high school, we took a personality test in health class. One of my results read, "You may marry an alcoholic because you think you can fix him." I remember being offended at first. After I thought about it, though, I realized there was a lot of truth in that statement. Not just for me, but for many girls.

Most girls love to see potential in guys. We dream about what he could be if we could just have the opportunity to influence him. His clothes. His hair. His personality. All of these things could be perfected if a girl could just be in a position of influence (like being his girlfriend) for one month or even a week.

Think about what girls used to do when they were little. They accessorized their Barbies—spending hours changing their outfits, doing their hair, placing them throughout the Barbie airplane, and then doing it all over again the next day. They dressed their cats and dogs up in baby clothes. They made crafts with glitter, paint, and obnoxious heart stickers. In summary, they took something that was okay and made it (in their eyes) great. And they think they can do that for YOU!

Do you have a quiet, shy personality? That's okay. When a girl enters your life, you will become the outgoing, friendly life of the party. You're not romantic? Don't worry. After going out with a girl for two short weeks, your friends will start calling you Romeo. That's what many girls think anyway.

A girl named Kelsey was interested in a guy. As girls often do, she called her friend for a personal consultation. She described the guy as "a little quiet, not really into fashion, but super nice and athletic." Her friend replied with one simple question, "Is he moldable and shapeable?" The answer was "Yeah, I think so." So she went to work. Suggesting a new haircut. Shopping with him for his new glasses.

> If you would like to know which Winnie the Pooh character you best resemble personality-wise, try the "100 Acre Personality Quiz" online!

my brain is a few years behind my body.

There's a little old lady who's lived in the same house for eighty-seven years (yes, she was born there, and she'll probably die there). But even more remarkable to me (because I'm like most guys) is Marion's 1977 Chevy Malibu parked in the garage. I've never known anyone to keep a car for so long.

In a way, I was fooled. What looked to me like an old car with one tire already in the junkyard was actually a car that had barely ever been driven. It had only 21,776 miles on it…just enough to drive to church every Sunday for thirty-three years. Marion's car—at least under the hood—was probably "newer" than what you or I drive today!

Teenage guys can fool you too, based on what is visible on the outside. When "Joe the Jock" walks down the hallway at Springfield School, many girls gush and blush at his manliness. A lot is happening in Joe's body—his shoulders are broadening, his voice is deepening, and his height is climbing higher and higher. Joe looks more like a man than ever before—he even shaves his peach fuzz once a week (whether he needs to or not!).

> Even before birth, the brains of boys develop slower than those of girls.
> Berger, 2003

That's not the whole story though. While Joe's body is changing faster than your Facebook status, his brain is progressing at a more conservative pace. In other words, what looks like a man is still in many ways just a boy.

Although Joe is strong, athletic, studly, and a ladies' man, at thirteen he may still play with action figure toys in the bathtub. His mental development is a few years behind his body. Couple that with the fact that most girls mature faster than guys, and you see how building a relationship can get pretty interesting.

When I was in seventh grade, my youth group went to a Minnesota Twins baseball game. Ninety-five middle schoolers in full-drama mode. I had a crush on Lisa, the prettiest thing in braces and bangs I'd ever seen. The problem was, my brain was still wired like a fifth

i may try to fix you. continued

Buying him a cute shirt for his birthday. Fixing him.

Maybe you've heard that guys like to fix things. If something is broke, you fix it. If you encounter a problem, you find a solution. If you're mad at a friend, you punch him and then go out for pizza. Girls fixing *a guy* is different. They want to take something that is good and make it fantastic. They want to take someone unnoticeable and make him someone who cannot be ignored!

So what can you do? If you're smart, you'll listen to her suggestions. We can all use a non-extreme makeover no matter who we are, right? But if a girl starts trying to change your personality, values, entire wardrobe, and God-given passions, you need to take a stand. You were created to be just who you are and a smart girl—the *right* girl—will know that and celebrate you—with all your quirks and uniquenesses...and maybe just a little more hair product.

. . . .

Try this in the next week:

1. Ask your mom, "Mom, were there things you wanted to change about dad when you first started dating or when you first got married?"
2. List three things you don't want to change about yourself—even if a girl is in the picture.
3. Think about this: What could be the negatives about allowing a girl to change some things about you?
4. What are some positive changes a girl has already brought to your life?

my brain is a few years behind my body. continued

grader. I wanted to flirt so badly. I wanted to capture Lisa's attention so she would know how much I liked her. And I wanted to impress all of the other guys. So I did what any seventh grade Romeo would do: I walked right over to Lisa's seat and poured my entire sixty-four ounce Mountain Dew on her lap.

She did not see this as flirting for some reason. Big surprise!

Girls, be warned: guys may fool you with their big muscles and baritone voices. Just like Marion's antique car, what's under the hood doesn't always match what's on the outside. Some will mature faster than others. Some will lag behind. Just be patient—they'll catch up in a few years. Until then, learning to dodge Moutain Dew may be a good thing to perfect.

. . . .

Try this in the next week:

1. Ask your dad to tell you about a time when he struggled to "grow up."
2. Next time a guy acts immature around you and hurts your feelings, just think to yourself, *His brain will catch up eventually.*
3. Remember: Don't take it personally! When guys act immature, it's really not about you.
4. Manage your expectations. Realize guys and girls mature differently and embrace those differences.

Trust in the LORD with all your heart and lean not on your own understanding; in all your ways submit to him, and he will make your paths straight.

PROVERBS 3:5–6

Everything that we see is a shadow cast by that which we do not see.

MARTIN LUTHER KING JR.

SECTION 2

....

what girls/guys
aren't thinking about

....

Debbie was always thinking while she drove her car. She thought about her make-up and hair. She thought about her favorite drink from Starbucks. But after eight months of neglecting to think about changing the engine oil, her engine blew up!

It's hard enough to understand what the opposite sex is thinking about, but it is just as important to understand what they're not thinking. If teenage guys aren't thinking beyond today, and if teenage girls aren't thinking of their relationships as short-term, that's a recipe for disaster.

Sometimes what we're not thinking about gets us in trouble and hurts us more than what we are thinking.

Guys and girls are put together differently. We speak different languages, feel different feelings, and think from unique perspectives. Factor in what we each *don't* think about, and it gets even more complicated. She's thinking romance, he's not; he's thinking of right now, she's thinking ever-after. She's thinking about how to get his attention, he can't stop thinking about that new double burger with bacon. See? Complicated.

But with a little insight and patience, it doesn't have to be. Guys and girls *can* understand each other. It just takes patience, practice, and little insight.

"There are days where we just feel like crap (for lack of a better word), and the last thing we want is for guys to be upset with us."

"We have mood swings."

that's what she said

"We are more emotional than we are anything else—and that's normal."

"Girls long to be loved and cared for, more than anything. And sometimes we do crazy things to try to get that feeling."

"We want to do something fun and active like play a game or sport... but still let the girl win."

"We aren't thinking of fixing them."

that's what he said ◄ • • •

"We want nothing more than for our girlfriends to be happy; even though we don't always know how to show it!"

Chapter 6

i am
who i am

i'm dramatic, and it causes problems.

i'm impulsive, and it causes problems.

i'm dramatic, and it causes problems.

According to the Bible, we were all created in the image of God. What a cool thing! Being created in His image means we have God qualities like creativity, intellect, and emotions—just to name a few. Can you imagine how boring life would be without emotions? Think about winning the championship game and not feeling excitement. Think about sitting in the middle of your pile of birthday presents and not being overwhelmed with happiness. Think about your favorite pet dying and not being able to experience sadness. Emotions are good. Emotions are a gift from God.

> To avoid the drama, I just hang out with the guys.
> Amy, fourteen years old

It seems God created most girls with approximately quadruple the emotions of guys. It may have something to do with preparing us to be moms some day, but I think it's mostly because God wanted to make guys and girls uniquely different, and this is one of the ways He chose to do it. In addition, he gave guys hair on their faces, girls the ability to do the splits, and guys the ability to spit incredibly long distances. (Guys may have gotten the better end of the deal!)

That extra dose of emotions typically ends up taking the form of drama. It seems that wherever you find two or more girls, you find a whole lot of drama. They can turn the simplest decision into a Broadway show. They have plenty of clothes in their closets, but "nothing to wear!" A girlfriend ignored her at a party and she now is dead to her. She got a C on a math test and now, in her mind, she'll will be working at McDonalds for the rest of her life. Drama. Add a few more girls into the mix and *Poof!* the drama increases. Do you know girls like that?

In the midst of this whirlwind of drama, people get hurt. Girls take sides, start rumors, excommunicate each other, and start grudges that will last for years. Unfortunately, the drama sucks in concerned parents, frustrated teachers, and caring youth workers. Meetings are held and plans are made to stop the hurt and try to mend.

Guys, beware! When they are at a party, on a retreat, or just

i'm impulsive, and it causes problems.

Robbie and his friends wanted to have fun. Dinner was over, and their parents were sitting inside visiting—way too boring for squirrely fourteen-year-olds! The guys built a snow fort on the edge of the yard, made ammunition out of snowballs and icicles, and went to war. After a while, war lost its edge and the guys came up with a new game: attacking passing motorists. The next car to drive down the street was pummeled with snowballs and ice chunks coming from all sides. The guys were the victors—they dominated the streets!

What the guys never considered was what would happen after their attack. The driver of the vehicle swerved and nearly hit a parked car. He then slammed on his brakes, screeched to a halt, and stormed out of the car. The guys ran for their lives, but the driver found their parents. Their humiliated parents, that is. The guys' impulsive decision to have fun backfired.

In their game of war, it's almost as if the guys' plan was "Ready! Fire! ...Aim!" They launched into action without knowing exactly what they were doing. Their adrenaline got the best of them, and they failed to think through the consequences of their actions.

Guys are more impulsive than girls. There is a scientific explanation for it. There is a section of our brains called the frontal lobe cortex. It's the part of the brain that affects the ability to reason, plan, discern, and think through cause-and-effect relationships. Girls' frontal lobe cortexes begin to develop earlier than guys' do. This part of the brain continues to develop until about age twenty-five for both genders, but guys start a few years later than girls.

> Impulsive: acting without forethought (sound familiar?).

We see evidence of guys' decision-making challenges all around us. Guys pay much higher car insurance premiums in their teens and early twenties because they are much more likely to speed, crash, and break the law than girls. Approximately 85 percent of teen violent

i'm dramatic, and it causes problems.
continued

hanging out with a group of friends, many girls will feed off each other's drama and become even more dramatic. Inconceivable, but true.

This is one of the main reasons girls are drawn to guys. Guys are nearly drama-free. Even though they have a closet full of clothes, guys typically choose the same jeans and one of three shirts to wear every day. If a guy friend ignores another guy, they usually just punch each other and go about their business. If he fails a test, a guy may be tempted to use a bad word or two, but most forget about it by lunch. Drama-free.

Girls do get tired of the drama. They long for friends who can just chill and not get worked up about everything. This is where you come in. Be your drama-free self and help girls to see life from a different perspective. Help them reign in the drama while encouraging them to use their emotions to cheer on, support, and inspire others.

. . . .

Try this in the next week:

When a girl who you hang out with starts to get dramatic, try to help her avoid the drama by gently offering one of the following suggestions:

1. "Why don't you pray about it? Then tell her what is bothering you."
2. "Let's go swing on the playground for awhile."
3. "I understand it's tough, but it will be better tomorrow."
4. "Have you ever thought of getting a punching bag?"

i'm impulsive, and it causes problems.
continued

crimes are committed by guys. And across America, girls graduate high school at a higher rate than guys. The simple fact is guys often "fire" before they aim. They don't think long-term or use the best judgment because they are still developing those skills and abilities.

It really gets interesting when guys try leading relationships with girls (they are also wired to be the leader in guy/girl relationships). He might say "I love you" without thinking through what that really means. An example is Reid and Nikki. When he told her that he loved her for the first time, Nikki stopped him dead in his tracks by saying, "Do you really mean that? Please think about what you're saying. Once you say that, you can't take it back." Nikki did not want her heart toyed with and helped Reid think through the magnitude of what he was saying.

When you're in a relationship with a guy, know that he may make decisions that bring physical, emotional, and spiritual consequences to both of you—decisions that he potentially hasn't thought through. It's good for you to know that he's on a path to growing up, just like you are, and he's not all the way there yet. Until then, try to be like Nikki and speak up. Just because a guy makes an impulsive decision doesn't mean you can't help him to understand the importance of his words and decisions.

. . . .

Try this in the next week:

When you notice a guy being impulsive and inappropriate, gently and quietly say something like:

"There are girls in the room, and you need to stop doing that."

"I love it when you are calm and pay attention to what is being said."

"Maybe you want to take some time to think and pray before you make a decision?"

"Act your age, not your shoe size!" (Okay, just kidding here.)

Chapter 7

what the future holds

i'm a hopeless romantic.

i'm not thinking of our future—I can't even spell marriage!

i'm a hopeless romantic.

Have you ever watched a Disney movie? Come on, be honest! Even guys are pulled in as Ariel transitions from life under the sea to land, or as Belle and the Beast have their snowball fight. You might be man enough to admit that you like Disney movies, but it's a fair bet they don't move you in the same way they move girls. From the time girls sit with pigtails on their heads and juice boxes in their hands watching those movies, their romantic nature is being formed. It's cute as they dress in their princess costumes and talk of their princes, but it's complicated (and even annoying) when it transfers to their teenage years and relationships.

If Snow White, Cinderella, and Mulan have men who come triumphantly to their rescue, that must mean the same will happen for "regular" girls, right? Obviously, you as a teenage guy will charge into her life, flowers in hand, hair blowing in the wind, ready to fight for her and say the things she has always wanted to hear. Fantasy, according to girls, should be their reality. More than likely, out of the things just listed, you might match up with one of them (if your mom will give you money to buy the flowers at the grocery store). That kind of fantasy puts you, as a guy, in a tough spot. How can you live up to further expectation?

> A "hopeless romantic" is in love with love.

A girl's dream date is a good example of their expectations. When asked what three elements would be a must in a dream date, teenage girls responded:

- Laughing a lot together (the number one answer!)
- Watching a sunset
- Having fun doing simple activities, like going to Target
- Easy conversation
- Laying out beneath the stars
- Holding hands
- Slow dancing
- Having him play the guitar

i'm not thinking of our future—
i can't even spell marriage!

During a high school class retreat, a group of girls sat in a room that overlooked the camp's lake and bonfire area where a group of guys were hanging out. For hours the girls talked about what they wanted out of their boyfriends—and their expectations sounded a lot like what most girls might hope for in marriage. They shared thoughts and dreams of marrying their boyfriends and living happily ever after.

What do you think the guys talked about down by the lake? They sure didn't talk about marrying their girlfriends. They probably told stupid jokes, tried to light their farts on fire, and had some kind of contest to outdo each other. There was probably not one guy down there who could even spell the word marriage.

Girls start thinking about marriage much earlier than guys. Little girls may like to play wedding dress-up when they are six years old. An old lace tablecloth makes the perfect wedding dress. Favorite stuffed animals are important members of the wedding party. And the family dog is usually the groom. Meanwhile, most six-year-old boys are busy squeezing peas up their noses and constructing guns from straws and plastic forks.

> The average age of a groom in the United States is twenty-nine.
>
> Brides Magazine

Angie wasn't really into make-believe—she started planning her wedding *for real* when she was twelve years old. All through her teenage years, Angie and her best friends built wedding kits in boxes they stored under their beds. These kits included pictures of dresses and floral arrangements cut from magazines, sample invitations and announcements, color swatches, lists of bridesmaids, and ideas for romantic honeymoon destinations around the world.

What are most guys thinking about during those same teenage years? They aren't thinking of their perfect wedding. They think incessantly about girls' looks and bodies. If they clip pictures out of magazines, it's more likely of scantily clad women than bridal couples

i'm a hopeless romantic. continued

How many of those elements would be included in *your* dream date? Notice, there is no mention of video games, pizza, kissing, driving fast, or anything sports related.

So, what is a good Christian guy to do? What do girls need you to do? It's natural for girls to hope for dream dates, but it's not realistic or fair to guys. What *really* matters to girls? It comes down to attention. It doesn't matter if you are sitting in the middle of the girl's family function, walking through the halls at school, sitting in youth group, or hanging out at the mall—if you are genuinely paying attention to a girl, you are doing what matters most. Give her eye contact, listen to her, ask her follow-up questions as you listen, notice her cute outfit (she put it together to impress you!), remember the things she likes, pray with her, and avoid texting other people when you're with her. If you can even pull off half of that list, you're doing great!

The truth is, girls will be hopeless romantics until Jesus comes back; however, you can still be seen as a dreamy guy by simply paying attention and treating her with honor and care. Watch, listen, and pray. Flowers and playing the guitar are added benefits—but not essential.

Try this in the next week:

1. Go back and watch a few Disney movies—try to watch from the perspective of a girl. What about the movies do you think feeds a girl's romantic nature?
2. Make an effort to pay attention to the females in your life—start with your mom, sister, or friend. Remember things they like, ask good questions, and compliment them on their outfits. It will make her day, and you'll feel better too!
3. If you are going out with a girl, try to come up with a date that would make both of you happy.

i'm not thinking of our future— i can't even spell marriage! continued

and wedding flowers. And years later when they finally do think about getting married, they are generally more excited about what will happen on their honeymoon than any other part of the wedding. Just as girls talk about how romantic marriage will be, many guys will talk with their buddies about their honeymoon fantasies.

So why do you need to know what they are thinking and not thinking about? The combination of girls' romantic notions and guys' impulsive nature can be a big problem. It's good for you to know that as you get more serious with a guy, that doesn't mean he's thinking about getting married. In fact, he's probably not thinking about your future because the part of his brain responsible for those kinds of thoughts is still in development. Sometimes girls allow guys too many liberties because they are thinking they will be together forever, when guys are generally thinking about right now. Be careful not to compromise your boundaries or give your heart away too fast under the dream that you've found your life-partner and soul mate. He's probably still trying to figure out how to spell marriage.

. . . .

Try this in the next week:

1. Make a list of three things (physically and emotionally) you want to save for your future husband.
2. Ask your dad, grandpa, or another man you know when he first started thinking seriously about marriage and why.

Chapter 8

how i get attention

> i use my body to my advantage.

> attention for the wrong reasons equals trouble.

i use my body to my advantage.

Warning: This gets serious. Read with caution...and depth. Girls were created with an innate need to be loved by a man. That need is intended to be filled by God the Father and a girl's earthly father. If girls don't engage in those two relationships (or aren't able to because their earthly father is absent or not a good man), they look to other guys to fill that space and need in their hearts.

One high school girl, for instance, had a dad that was pretty much a jerk. He didn't talk to her much, and when he did his words were cutting and negative. Even though he treated her so poorly, she desperately wanted to please him and make him happy. She would clean the house, speak respectfully, make meals for the family, and do her homework. He still just criticized. Finally, subconsciously, she turned from her dad to guys at school. The guys she chose (or that chose her) were not so great, but she drank in their attention and physical affection because it was "filling" that need she had to be loved.

. . . .

The message to girls from magazines, TV shows, and movies is "more cleavage, more attention."

. . . .

One of the major ways girls try to gain that attention from guys is by using their bodies. Even though I Corinthians 6:19 clearly states that our bodies are not our own, but were bought at a price, society has told girls that their bodies are theirs to be used however they choose. There was an interview with one female celebrity where she basically said, "I've worked hard for this body! I can do whatever I want with it!" And many girls do. They dress in ways that are provocative (showing lots of skin, leg, and chest). They grind at school dances. They take sexy pictures of themselves in bikinis or tank tops and post them on Facebook.

Let's be honest, guys. When a girl posts sexy photos or dances in a suggestive way, guys take notice. Some guys pay more attention to her. Some will ask her out. Some will want to be physical

attention for the wrong reasons equals trouble.

Andrew didn't have friends. He struggled to fit in because he talked and dressed funny. Socially, he lagged behind because he didn't spend a lot of time with kids his age. Andrew was the butt of jokes and target of bullies.

Andrew so desperately wanted to fit in, he tried to win friends by buying them treats. Most days at school he used his meal card to buy smoothies for other students. At first he thought the guys on the football team really wanted to be his friends. They gave him attention... at least while he bought their treats. But then the guys would take their smoothies and move on to their real friends and Andrew would be left at his lunch table alone.

A relationship built on being used is phony and fake—it's not real. Some guys don't mind phony if it feels good and gets them what they want—especially when it comes to girls.

> I know the kind of attention girls like, and I'll give it to them to get what I want.
>
> Jason, fifteen years old.

Tenth-grader Jason says it this way, "I know the kind of attention girls like, and I'll give it to them to get what I want." Jason knows that if he is attentive to his girlfriend she will likely give him more of the attention he wants.

Make no mistake, Jason's way of thinking is not right. You don't deserve to be manipulated for any guy's physical pleasure. If you want to be sure a guy's intentions are true, hold back on becoming physical and see how the relationship develops.

Guys and girls both crave attention, but they want it in different ways:

Most guys think:
- Notice my muscles (and squeeze them!)
- Be my biggest fan (and keep your eyes on me while I do my thing)
- The more we do physically, the better
- Don't talk so much
- You're part of my world

i use my body to my advantage. continued

with her. Don't fall into that trap! Do what the Bible says and, "Run from sexual sin! No other sin so clearly affects the body as this one does. For sexual immorality is a sin against your own body" (1 Corinthians 6:18 NLT).

The sad thing about girls using their bodies to their advantage is that it's not really an advantage at all. A girl who uses her body to get the attention from guys usually does so because she isn't confident in who she was created to be. She is insecure about who she is and uses her body to cover up that insecurity. The tragic end result is that when a guy pays attention to or likes a girl because of her body, he doesn't really like the girl. He's just lusting after her body (which according to the Bible is a sin). This "wrong attention," in turn, makes her even more insecure about herself. It leads her to ask, "Why can't a guy love me for who I am?" Unfortunately, that's a question she'll probably be trying to answer the rest of her life. See? It is not an advantage at all.

You can help build self-esteem and confidence in your girl friends by giving them a different kind of attention—attention to their words, their smiles, their compassion, their purity, or their ability to beat you at arm wrestling!

. . . .

Try this in the next week:

1. When you are getting to know a girl, evaluate what her relationship is like with her dad. If it's a neutral or negative relationship, be aware that she may be looking to you to fill her need for a father's love. Show her compassion and treat her with respect.

2. Let your friends that are girls know that you care about who they are—point out their non-physical characteristics that you value.

3. If you know a girl in your school who uses her body for attention, pray for her and ask that God would show her where her true value comes from.

**attention for the wrong
reasons equals trouble.** continued

Most girls think:
- Notice that I'm pretty (and tell me)
- Think about me often (and let me know that you do)
- I just want to be close to you
- Listen to me and remember what I say
- You are my world

Girls, this message may be new to you: sometimes guys know what you want and they play along to get more of what they want. And many times girls employ the same strategy. Either way, it leaves you with a phony relationship where you're getting used. Have patience and build trust. Wait for the guy who refuses to use your need for attention against you.

There are guys out there focused on your character and on keeping you safe. Their attention is pure and genuine and not at all a strategy to use you. Don't get yourself in trouble by trying so hard to attract anyone that you attract the wrong one. You should expect a man to respect and honor you and settle for nothing less.

Try this in the next week:

1. Go to one of your guy friend's games. Get there on time—cheer for him—pay attention to what's going on all game long—and after the game, find him, hug him, and tell him how great he did. How does he respond?
2. If you are going out with a guy who doesn't care about you, break up with him. You deserve better. You deserve someone who cares about you for who you are—not for what you give him or because of his attraction to your body.

Chapter 9

long-term purity

i'm not thinking this is short-term.

i'm not thinking about protecting your purity.

i'm not thinking this is short-term.

Most little girls dream of being married by age four. It starts with putting the living room drapes over her head and "walking down the aisle with her veil on." It's intensified when she is asked by her older cousin to be the flower girl in her wedding. She gets to be fitted for her own little bride-like dress and walk down a real aisle with flowers in her hair. She revels in the day, the attention, and the experience. It's like she's been a bride in training since she was in preschool!

So when you ask her out, she is at a very different place than you. You're thinking she's cute and makes you feel funny inside. She more than likely is thinking you are the one chosen for her since the beginning of time. She says yes to your invitation with long-term hopes, plans, and expectations. Kind of scary, huh?

Because she's seeing your relationship as long-term, she has great expectations. She assumes you will hang out a lot. She expects that you would remember important things like her birthday, the date you met, her locker combo, her favorite nail polish color, and how many sit-ups she could do in a minute three weeks ago.

When she thinks of a relationship as long-term (like leading to marriage), she is also more willing to give herself physically. Many girls at the end of a relationship have cried in regret for what they gave of themselves sexually while dating. When asked why they allowed things to go that far, they responded with "I thought he was the one." Girls who are thinking long-term sometimes see marriage in the future of every relationship and believe that being sexual is okay as long as marriage is the end goal.

This theory actually contradicts what the Bible says about sex. Hebrews 13:4 warns, "Marriage should be honored by all, and the marriage bed kept pure, for God will judge the adulterer and all the sexually immoral." Think about what the word "pure" means in the scientific world. It matches words like uncontaminated, untouched,

> One of the most popular Halloween costumes for young girls is a beautiful bride.

i'm not thinking about protecting your purity.

What can you do with a boyfriend that you can't do with a friend? Before you answer, here's the catch—you have to think of something that has nothing to do with being physical. What can you come up with?

Some people would say that with a boyfriend you can:

- Share deep, personal feelings
- Spend lots of time together
- Count on him to be there for you
- Get to know him even better
- Do fun activities together

While everything in the list above is true—you can do those things with boyfriends—everything in that list is also possible with friends. It's actually pretty difficult to think of activities that are unique boyfriend-only activities outside of physical affection.

Follow the logic for a moment. No one really likes going to job interviews. They're stressful and nerve-racking. But we really like having a job. The job interview is a means to get the job. So we only pursue job interviews when we are ready for a new job. Do you see where this is going?

> **Over 40 percent of young teens in the United States have lost their virginity by the age of fourteen.**
> The New York Academy of Medicine

What if we viewed dating as a means to finding a spouse? Wouldn't that mean you start dating when you feel ready for that kind of a commitment? Most people are not seriously looking for a spouse in their teens. So why are they dating? That could seem as silly as going to job interviews years before actually being ready for a job. Think of the pressure, stress, and expectations we put on ourselves to be involved in dating relationships, not to mention the physical expectations that are eventually added to most relationships.

Becky's boyfriend pressured her to have sex. She made him say he loved her and promise that he meant it. But a few weeks later they weren't together anymore. Becky was crushed that she gave away

i'm not thinking this is short-term.

continued

clean, flawless, and unblemished. Translation: when you reach your marriage bed, your sexual past should be uncontaminated and clean. That passage makes no exception for couples who think they're going to get married. It is what it is.

Guys, unlike girls, probably aren't thinking long-term when you ask someone out in high school. But you need to always be thinking long-term if purity is your goal. Be thoughtful in asking a girl out. What are your intentions? What is your motivation? If it's just for fun, then skip it. She deserves more and so do you.

If you're not thinking in the long-term, consider friendship as a great alternative. The only true difference between dating and a friendship is the physical piece. As friends, you can spend time together, get to know one another, and have great conversations. There is no hurry to advance the relationship.

If you do have a girlfriend, make sure you set physical boundaries together as a couple—which by the way should be done the first week of dating. Keep the word *pure* in mind. What can you do to assure that you, as a couple, will be honoring of God's hope and plan for your physical relationship and future?

. . . .

Try this in the next week:
1. Read Hebrews 13:4 and journal about what that would look like in a physical, dating relationship.
2. Read 1 Thessalonians 4:3–5. What does it mean to be "sanctified" in your sexual relationships?
3. Ask the Lord to help you honor girls as you relate with them day-to-day.

i'm not thinking about protecting your purity. continued

so much of her heart and body to a guy before marriage. He wasn't thinking of staying together for the long-term. He was thinking of the moment.

Unfortunately, most of guys you date in junior high or high school aren't thinking about your purity. They're not thinking about marriage. And they're not thinking about saving their own purity for marriage (either physical or emotional). Many are not even sure why they're dating because they haven't taken the time to think it through. Dating is often unintentional. But it is a big deal, and it's dangerous to enter into it unless you are honest about your intentions.

If you're totally honest with yourself, you'll probably agree that most teens start dating before they really think much about it. You like someone and you start going out. But remember, until you are ready to find a husband (many years from now), there's nothing you can do with a boyfriend that you can't also do with a friend. Protect your purity and his. Enjoy friendship. Maybe serious dating is something that can wait.

. . . .

Try this in the next week:

1. Ask yourself "What's my purpose in dating?" If it's not leading you down the road to marriage, where is it leading you?
2. What pressure does dating bring (both physically and emotionally) that you don't need to deal with right now?

This is my prayer: that your love may abound more and more in knowledge and depth of insight, so that you may be able to discern what is best and may be pure and blameless for the day of Christ, filled with the fruit of righteousness that comes through Jesus Christ— to the glory and praise of God.

PHILIPPIANS 1:9–11

The language of friendship is not words, but meanings.

HENRY DAVID THOREAU

SECTION 3

....

what girls/guys won't tell you

....

Our insecurities often keep us from wearing our feelings on our sleeves. Guys try as hard as they can to look cool and confident, but sometimes come across as cocky jerks. Girls become mean (usually to one another) as a strategy to hide their own insecurities from being revealed. It just feels too vulnerable to be real all the time, so we hide behind the masks we create.

The next five chapters take a closer look at what girls and guys won't tell each other. Sometimes the secret is kept on purpose to cover insecurities. But other times, girls and guys won't tell about parts of themselves because they're still trying to figure themselves out.

Love is a big idea. Just bringing it up in conversation reveals a lot about how important it is. Everyone has an opinion. But what is not said about it is just as revealing. You're about to learn what girls and guys won't tell you about love and relationships: It's complicated and easily misinterpreted. So read with an open mind and get an inside look into how the opposite sex thinks.

"When guys ask you for advice and value your input, when they bring their problems to you because they want to hear what you have to say, it makes you feel respected."

"We feel respected when you truly listen to us, instead of just hearing us."

**that's what
she said**

"It means a lot to know you trust me, and that you really see me!"

"There's such thing as too much teasing. There's a line between flirting and just being mean."

"We feel respected when they aren't on their phone all the time when we talk to them."

"We don't always understand things."

that's what he said ◄ • • • •

"Why do so many beautiful girls think they're ugly? We hate that."

"It means a lot when she can close her mouth to listen to me."

Chapter 10

the meaning of words

i talk too much.

i can be insensitive and hurtful.

I talk too much.

Have you ever sat back on a bus, in a classroom, or at a game and marveled at how much girls talk? It seems like they can talk about anything, right? Clothes, make-up, hair, kitties—it doesn't matter the topic, girls will talk about it…often really fast and usually for a long time!

It's not just your imagination. Studies have been done, and the results are amazing—in an average day, guys use 7,000 words (that doesn't include grunts!). Girls, on the other extreme, speak or text 20,000 words a day! Almost three times more words than you use!

> **Girls communicate an average of 20,000 words a day—13,000 more than guys!**

How does that happen? Doesn't the Bible say that we all were created in the image of God? It sure does—in Genesis, chapter one—but check out the last part: "So God created mankind in his own image, in the image of God he created them; *male and female he created them*" (verse 12, emphasis added). Our creative God decided to mix it up a bit and make guys and girls different. Much of God's reasoning for the differences between guys and girls will remain a mystery, but we do know that most of the differences stem from the brain. One psychiatrist even says that when a girl engages in talking, a chemical is released in her brain that gives her a rush similar to taking drugs. Talking is addictive for girls!

What should you do if you are a friend or boyfriend to one of these 20,000-word speakers? Well, being a good listener would be a great start! One things girls love almost as much as talking with other girls is talking with (or at!) a guy who will actively listen. Engage with her—give her eye contact, nod your head, and ask her follow-up questions. You will help her to feel valued and cared for. And, bonus, she'll think you're amazing!

Honestly, sometimes we girls talk simply because we're unsettled. Insecurity turns into endless chatter. Anxiety comes out in a constant stream of words. We don't know how else to handle it, so we default

I can be insensitive and hurtful.

Mark didn't just want me to go snowboarding with him—Mark wanted to teach me how to snowboard. He was a fifteen-year-old snowboarding maniac with no fear. And I was ten years older with enough fear for the two of us!

If you've ever been to a real mountain for winter recreation, you might laugh at the little hill we were on. Mark and I braved the slopes on what some might call bumps, but they looked huge to me. I was terrified.

Three hours on the bunny hill proved to be my limit. After the third time my board turned sideways, gripped the ground, and whipped me crashing on my head, I decided snowboarding was too painful and too scary. For the rest of the day, I sipped hot cocoa in the chalet and nursed my wounded head.

The experience of learning how to snowboard reminds me of how guys learn to talk to girls. They fall and fall and fall, and get hurt. Sometimes the people around them get hurt too. Maybe you've been hurt by careless teasing or insensitive words from a guy.

For instance, a group of high school friends was hanging out—guys and girls. When the pizza was delivered, Katie reached for two slices. Matt, normally a kind, decent guy, warned Katie, "Put that back—or it will go straight to your hips!"

Guys communicate 7,000 words a day—13,000 less than girls!

You may wonder what Matt was thinking to say something like that. He was probably thinking, "More food for me!" Katie was pretty and thin and she was also a good friend of Matt's. He did not mean to hurt her feelings or wound her self-esteem. He momentarily had a lapse of judgment and spoke hurting, insensitive words. He had no idea that Katie had issues with food and self-image already—he was just goofing around.

Guys at this age are just learning how to talk to girls and are often insensitive and hurtful. They are beginning to learn the sport of guy/girl communication but there are going to be lots of falls along the

I talk too much. continued

to the thing we know how to do—talk. So if you think a girl is talking due to insecurity, what should you do? If you know the girl well, you could say something like, "Hey, is everything okay?"

Let's be real, though, there will be times when a girl will wear you out with all her talking. This is where girl time and guy time come in. If you are dating a girl, make sure she has time with other girls. She will use a good amount of her words on them and not expect you to talk an unreasonable amount when you are together. Just remember, her use of words is normal, so try to accept them with attentive ears and a kind heart.

. . . .

Try this in the next week:

If you have a girl you're close to, these tips might help your relationship:

1. If you're going to be spending time (or chatting on the phone or online) with her later in the day, save some of your 7,000 words for her.
2. When in doubt, ask a question or say, "Tell me more about that."
3. Ask the Lord to help you be a good listener.
4. Think of topics that you both have an interest in and focus on those.

I can be insensitive and hurtful. continued

way. Chances are you will get hurt more than once.

It may be helpful to understand where guys are coming from. Most guys play, hit, and shoot. They are used to coaches and other leaders barking orders at them and delivering messages without much of a filter. These guys call it like they see it and often speak before they think. They love to tease each other. They are rough and playful in their communication. And they mask insecurities about themselves with bravado and cockiness.

Something starts to happen as a guy gets older, though. He becomes more aware of what impresses you and he really wants to win your approval and affection. It can be frustrating and embarrassing for him when he trips over his words. It can feel overwhelming if he feels like he is constantly disappointing you.

You can model good communication and kindness in words. Be gracious and cut guys some slack as they learn. Just like learning to snowboard, learning to talk with girls can be painful at times! But with a little guidance and practice, both of you will be gliding along like pros in no time.

. . . .

Try this in the next week:

Next time you hear a guy say something that's hurtful or inappropriate, kindly help him with a simple response, like:

1. "I don't like it when you joke about that."
2. "Please don't talk that way around me."
3. "You're saying hurtful words, and I'd like you to stop."

Chapter 11

it's all about me

i'm mean.

i'm selfish.

i'm mean.

It may be hard to see at first glance, but many girls are mean. Sure, when you look at them, they're smiling, smelling good, laughing, shopping, and flipping their hair. In the depths of their hearts, though, many are mean.

There are an abundance of stories from teenage girls that paint a good picture of mean! How about this one: Kelsey started the first day of her new middle school, excited to meet new people and have new opportunities. Unfortunately, she was made fun of the first day. Kids made fun of her weight and called her a "Bible-banger" because they knew she came from a private, Christian school. It was awful, but Kelsey had one friend in the class, Sarah. She had met Sarah at church, and they were friends. That helps, right? Having at least one friend? During those first, tough months, Kelsey hung out with Sarah and all her friends.

> **"She's fabulous, but she's evil."**
> Damian, from the movie *Mean Girls*

Life seemed to get a little better until she received an eight-page note from Sarah. The note, with degrading drawings in the margins of the paper, told Kelsey she was fat, the girls were ashamed to be seen with her, and never wanted to be her friends again. Not only did Sarah sign the note, but she brought it to all the other girls in the class and they signed it too—agreeing with all that Sarah had written about Kelsey.

The main reason teenage girls are mean is because they are doing whatever it takes to advance themselves socially. It's a different system than guys are used to—it doesn't draw from what a girl does on the court or how much she can bench in the weight room or how well she plays the guitar. It has more to do with an image they can spin—the image of physical beauty, social power, and control of guys. It appears most girls would give anything to have their social status be determined by the weight they could benchpress—life would be much simpler that way.

The two primary weapons of a girl's meanness are words and

i'm selfish.

The moment a baby is born he or she fusses and cries when hungry, tired, or bored. They are born wanting only to have their needs taken care of and now! Babies by nature are selfish.

Toddlers aren't much better. They throw old toys aside and move on to the new toy...until they see another toddler pick up the first toy. When that happens, they will push, pull, or rip it away. They want what they want. Toddlers are selfish.

Kids are selfish too. They run for the front of lunch lines as though there's not enough food to go around. They want all your attention. They want to be first down the slide.

Sarah learned this the hard way. It seems like Sarah has had a crush on Matt forever. In elementary school she thought he was the cutest boy on the playground. In middle school she dreamed about marrying him. In high school they became good friends (strictly platonic friends in his mind). Sarah invited Matt to the Sadie Hawkins dance and it was a dream come true for her when he said yes.

The night of the dance, Matt was anything but Prince Charming. He pulled his car into her driveway and honked the horn. (Sarah's dad didn't let her go outside until Matt used his manners and came to the front door.) Matt eventually swaggered up the front walk, twirling a single rose in his hand. When Sarah opened the door, Matt said, "Here, my mom got this flower for you."

The night went from bad to worse at every turn. Matt and a buddy rode in the front seats and Sarah rode in the back of the car. Matt sat with his guy friends and stuffed his face at Old

Selfishness naturally results in a disregard for others.

Country Buffet while Sarah wondered when their date would truly begin. Sarah never had a slow dance that night because Matt left the dance floor to play basketball with his friends on the other side of the gym. Eventually, he returned only to ask Sarah if she could find another ride home. He wanted to leave with his buddies to go home and play video games!

i'm mean. continued

manipulation. In the book of James chapter three, the tongue is de-scribed as a "restless evil, full of deadly poison" (verse 8). The tongue is a small part of the body, but like a small spark in the middle of a forest, it can do great damage. Sadly, in order for girls to advance socially, some mistakenly believe they need to cut other people down. Their words are quick, cutting, and heard by many. Mass texts. Face-book posts. Rumors whispered. The crazy part is, although many of these girls look strong and confident on the surface, they are sad, insecure, and often falling apart inside.

A great partner in crime to an evil tongue is manipulation. Many girls meanly manipulate situations and others in order to advance themselves. So, if it's most advantageous for her to date you (because you are connected to the cool group of guys she wants to be associ-ated with), she may do what she needs to do to seduce you. It doesn't matter if her best friend likes you. It really doesn't even matter if *she* likes you. This particular girl is mean.

Teenage girls may seem sweet and innocent at first glance, but they can have a mean streak. Help them by not buying into it. They can only manipulate you if you let them. Open your eyes and don't follow mean girls' actions. You can make a difference!

• •

Try this in the next week:
1. Identify the girls in your life who don't give into meanness and let them know you notice and appreciate their difference.
2. Don't let yourself get caught up in a girl's meanness—say things like, "Hey, I don't want to hear that. Let's talk about something else," or "I like her and will talk to her."
3. Pray for the girls in your life—asking God to soften their hearts and increase their love for others.

i'm selfish. continued

The craziest part of this true story is that Matt was and is an awesome guy. In fact, if you flash forward a few years to today, he's the kind of godly, thoughtful guy you'd want to marry. But when he was sixteen, his selfishness was turbo charged. He wasn't thinking at all about Sarah the night of the dance—he was only thinking about his fun.

Guys simply develop slower than girls develop. They don't mean to be jerks—they're just not fully aware of how their actions make other people feel, especially girls.

Selfishness at its worst is when a guy pushes up against your physical boundaries. He may disguise it in the name of love or passion, but you need to see it for what is really is: selfishness. And you need to call it out so he knows you know.

The journey from selfish to selfless is long and ongoing. But be careful not to tie yourself to anyone who isn't at least making his way down that road. Guys don't like to disappoint, so remember, your patience will encourage him to keep on trying.

• •

Try this in the next week:

1. Ask someone close to you if they see a selfish streak in you. If so, in what areas? We're all works in progress!
2. When you see a guy friend being selfish, point out people that need help or other situations outside of his life. Help him think beyond himself.
3. Pray for the guys in your life—asking God to make them more aware of what is happening in the lives of other people and how his selfishness can affect them.

Chapter 12

what you think matters

strength is great, but it doesn't top my list.

i'm insecure about what you think of me.

strength is great, but it doesn't top my list.

Walking into a weight room and observing its inhabitants is amusing. It's a different world than the rest of the school, club, or gym. Surrounded by clumps of metal and mirrors, guys grunt, sweat, and stare at themselves. Sure it's hard *not* to stare at themselves when enclosed with mirrors, but it's still amusing. Their eyes are drawn to their rippling biceps as they curl and their tightening quads as they squat. Most guys are into physical strength.

A guy's focus on strength starts young. Nearly every time I'm around my young nephews, they yell, "Hey! Watch this!" as they lift a five-pound weight, the cat, their younger brother, or anything else they think will showcase their growing power. I always respond as expected, "Wow! You are so strong!" Their big smiles as they say, "I know!" shows the value of that strength.

In our sports-oriented culture, you will find more girls in the guy-dominated gym or weight room than you have at any other time in American history. A girl's attention to physical strength, however, differs in comparison to a guy's. Girls want to be fit, lean, athletic, and toned. It is a rare girl who desires to have mass and bulging muscles.

> A guy's natural response when a girl grabs his arm is to flex his bicep to show his strength.

When a girl is considering a guy, strength is appreciated, but it's not at the top of her list. She appreciates strength because she loves to feel physically protected by a guy. She wants to be confident that if she is walking down a dark alley with a guy, he can bring the smackdown on any attacker or cocky teenage kid. She likes that he can open her nail polish bottle that won't budge in her hands. She also admires the way his arms look in a tight T-shirt. But when matched up with the really important things, physical strength fades in comparison.

As females, girls are looking for a different kind of strength. They're more into emotional strength. Are you aware of your feelings? Do you have guts enough to identify those feelings and share

i'm insecure about what you think of me.

The house was too quiet for having two teenage guys in it—it must mean trouble. When nobody else was home, Michael and his friend secretly started watching an X-rated movie they had found in his big brother's room. But when his parents explored the reason for a quiet house, the guys were caught.

Michael couldn't speak without crying—nothing felt worse than disappointing his dad. He was a pure-minded, thirteen-year-old guy, free from adolescent urges and curiosities. He hadn't even wanted to watch an X-rated movie, but it was their first time hanging out and he didn't want to disappoint his new friend. Michael was so insecure about fitting in that he didn't want to be different.

> **Men have always had insecurities; they just don't talk about them like women do.**
> CNN Living

Most guys struggle with insecurity to some degree. They're concerned about what their friends think more than anyone else. They may appear to be confident or even cocky, but inside they want to be accepted and fit in just as much as anyone. Peer pressure is pretty strong among guys. They want to live up to unrealistic expectations the world has, like:

- Real men are tough.
- Real men are sexually experienced.
- Real men are great athletes.
- Real men are confident.
- Real men are successful (and earn lots of money).

Guys are also insecure about what girls think of them. Girls have their secret meetings in bathrooms and whisper and giggle just enough to leave guys a bit paranoid. They respond by trying to impress you. That's where it gets tricky, because what impresses guys generally isn't the same as what impresses girls.

Next time a guy comes across as being a cocky jerk, remember that he may be overcompensating for being insecure. He may be trying to impress you but just doesn't know how. In his nervousness, he will default back to the things he thinks he's supposed to say and

strength is great, but it doesn't top my list. continued

them with us? Do those feelings expand beyond anger and frustration? Are you in tune with me enough to sense when I'm struggling and ask me about it? Give them a guy like that, and girls don't care if he has ever set foot in a weight room.

They also appreciate strength of character. Do you act the same way around your parents as you do around your school buddies? Are you trustworthy? Do you tell the truth even if it may cause trouble for you? Do you desire to live a life that is godly and pure? Are you a loyal and faithful friend? Do you respect me and my sexual boundaries? They'll take a guy like that over a PX90 pro any day of the week.

So, what kind of strength do you have? Have you thought about building your inner strength? Your character? Your death grip on purity? You may just find that inner strength is at the top of her list.

· ·

Try this in the next week:

1. Compare the time you spend in the gym to the time you spend developing your character. Which one is greater?
2. Spend some time reflecting on your emotional maturity. You might even want to try journaling or putting thoughts in a personal blog.
3. Ask your parents or a trusted adult, "Am I trustworthy? Why or why not?"

i'm insecure about
what you think of me. continued

do—the stuff that normally only impresses other guys, like showing their muscles or leaving a dance to show off their basketball skills.

Guys like to tell girls a lot about what they *do* rather than who they *are*. So while you're waiting for him to pour out his feelings, he'll be working really hard to impress you with sports stats or car talk.

Guys want your approval or they wouldn't try to impress you. And sometimes they'll do things that are out of character or even stupid because they want to live up to the "real man" ideas that are being fed to them. Your words are powerful enough to encourage or crush him. Use them wisely.

. . . .

Try this in the next week:

Affirm a guy friend with your words. Tell him something you really believe about him, like:

1. "You have the best smile!"
2. "I like it when you open the door for me—you're such a gentleman."
3. "My friends and I respect you so much."
4. "I always have fun when you're around."
5. "I'm lucky to have you for a friend."

Chapter 13

no baggage needed

don't make me rent a u-haul.

when I'm ready to be serious, i don't want baggage.

don't make me rent a u-haul.

Hopefully, as you've been reading, you've picked up on the sense that the majority of girls are emotional creatures. We feel things deeply and with great force—especially when those feelings are connected to a physical relationship. This is one of the main reasons why girls are encouraged to hold off on dating and being physical as long as possible.

Imagine the consequences of not following this wise advice. A twelve-year-old girl, overwhelmed by all the new guys in her middle school, goes out with the first guy who asks her. Desperately wanting to be liked by him, she kisses him within a week. He's happy and so is she. Within a month, they are sneaking away from their friends to make-out. But on that dreadful Monday, after a serious make-out session, he sends a message through his buddy that he wants to break up. She's devastated and feels used. She is certain she will not let that happen again.

> The earlier a girl starts dating, the more emotional baggage she will carry into her relationships.

After a month or so, though, she notices another guy in her gym class. He seems different. After flirting with him during the volleyball unit, she asks him out through a text and his reply makes them a couple. He makes her heart beat like crazy just by touching her arm! He invites her over to hang out with a bunch of friends, but none of them showed up, so they ended up by themselves in the basement. It was the perfect opportunity to start kissing, touching, and going further than she had gone with the other guy. She was uncertain until he told her she was the most beautiful girl he'd ever seen. Later that month, she broke up with him to go out with a guy she had met over spring break.

Unfortunately, that only covered about three-fourths of her seventh grade year. Now, play that pattern out over the next five years, until she's a senior in high school. She, more than likely, will have gone out with at least fifteen more guys, going further and further sexually

when I'm ready to be serious, i don't want baggage.

There comes a day for most guys when they finally grow up. That doesn't mean they're complete, and it doesn't mean they're fully mature. It means they've left boyhood behind and have started thinking and acting like a man.

Acting like a man doesn't have anything to do with the messages we see all around us. Becoming a man is actually a counter-cultural way of living. The world says men have sex with lots of women. A real man saves himself for one woman—his wife. The world says men make lots of money. A real man thinks more about the money he shares than the money he makes. The world says men are rough and tough. A real man has a heart for God.

Guys who think the way the world tells them to think like to party and hook up with girls. When a guy becomes serious about life and love, something starts to change in his heart. When he's ready to find a wife and settle down, he's rarely attracted to a girl with a lot of baggage.

What's baggage? Baggage is the stuff you'd rather not bring from one relationship to the next. Baggage that really stinks comes from the stuff girls do with their bodies to get guys' attention. There's usually a time when it is super exciting for a guy to know that a girl will let a guy touch her body. Guys often believe the lie that they can just have fun today and it doesn't really matter what they do. But when they're ready to be serious, they don't want to settle for an experienced girl. They want to find someone they can respect as a wife and mother of their future children.

> The average size of carry-on luggage allowed on a flight is twenty-two inches by fourteen inches.

Most guys carry an enormous double standard around with them. According to how these guys think, the same reputation that could make a girl popular in high school ("she'll go all the way") could keep her from being wife material later. They value the experience they've had with girls, but they want to settle down with a girl they see as

don't make me rent a u-haul. continued

with each one. Each kiss and each touch will make the break-ups even more emotionally disappointing—her expectations, her regrets, her decreasing self-respect becoming pieces of emotional luggage that she has to pack up at the end of each relationship. When she heads off for her first year in college, she'll need to rent TWO U-Haul trailers—one for her shoes and clothes and the other for all the emotional baggage she's accumulated over her teenage years.

Although most of the responsibility for that baggage lies with the girl and her choices, you have great influence. Make sure none of the baggage she carries around was packed by you. A girl longs to be cared for, loved, and protected. When you do that well with the girls in your world, you help them to limit their baggage. That's a win-win for both of you!

. . . .

Try this in the next week:

1. Each time you see a suitcase, U-Haul truck, or moving van, remember the emotional baggage girls acquire in relationships.
2. Read Proverbs 4:23. Pray about how you can protect your heart and any girl date.
3. Treat each girl in your life with kindness and care.

when I'm ready to be serious, i don't want baggage. continued

sexually pure. It's as absurd as an obese man who doesn't take care of himself insisting on marrying a fitness instructor.

What do they consider baggage? Baggage is the physical and emotional stuff from previous relationships. Whether it's physical experience (like many guys want) or serious emotional relationships (like many girls want), it results in baggage you pack up and carry with you for a long time. How many married people do you know who started dating their spouse in junior high or high school? It happens, but not all that often. Most likely the person you're interested in today is not the person you'll end up with for good. Do you really want to be a baggage carrier?

As you date, consider dating with the end in mind. What's the point of dating? You could make a case that dating is a chance for you to get to know a guy well enough to see if there's a future with him. If there is, you continue to invest. But beyond that, dating can be a breeding ground for baggage. If you are just wanting to have fun and share a pure, innocent relationship with a guy, establish and keep boundaries. Make sure you know which kind of relationship you are in and keep it baggage-free.

. . . .

Try this in the next week:

1. Have you compromised your standards for a guy? Be real with a trusted adult or mentor and unpack that baggage.
2. Ask yourself, "Is my heart telling me to make a change as I move forward in this relationship?"

Chapter 14

he loves me, he loves me not

i'll mistake your infatuation for love.

don't mistake my infatuation for love.

i'll mistake your infatuation for love.

Have you ever been infatuated with something? Consumed by the desire to have, possess, or own a thing? A lot of guys are infatuated with cars, electronics, power, and money. They like how these things make them feel. Cars offer status. Electronics keep them connected and entertained. Money makes them feel powerful. Whatever a guy is into at the time is where he devotes his time and energy. When he gets bored with it, he moves on to something else.

Unfortunately, some guys are infatuated with girls. They like how girls make them feel, what girls might give them physically, and the status they bring. Guys aren't usually thinking of love or commitment. Most are just excited about having someone to cheer them on at games or watch them dominate video games in their buddy's basement.

Most girls, however, translate a guy's actions in a different way. When you wave at her in the stands from the basketball court, her heart skips a beat. When she wears your jersey, she feels a deep connection to you. In her mind, you would never think of her as a thing. You care about her and want a future with her. More than likely, she thinks she's falling in love with you, while you may be just waiting for the next time you get to make-out with her.

> If you are giving something up, you must replace it with something else in order to be successful.

It's important for girls to know the difference between infatuation and intimacy. To protect their hearts, we encourage girls to try two different tests. One is called the "thirty-day, no-touch test." It's actually a great test for anyone in a relationship, but especially for a girl who wonders if she is the object of simple infatuation. For thirty days, she and her boyfriend are not to have any physical contact—no holding hands, kissing, or arms around each other. One of three things will happen:

1. They won't be able to make it thirty days without touching, indicating that their relationship was too focused on the physical.

don't mistake my infatuation for love.

A positive trait of teenage guys is their excitement and enthusiasm. A guy who learns how to waterski could spend all day in the water without getting cold or tired. When a new electronic gaming system goes on sale, guys will camp outside overnight to be the first in line. Some actually look forward to two-a-days and extra practices because that means the sport season is back in full swing. In general, guys play hard, sleep hard, and work hard.

Another way to say it is that guys can be all-in or all-out. They can get tunnel vision and be hyper-focused on one thing at a time. They *love* sports, trucks, guns, cars, big TVs, and even basketball shoes. Guys know how to love things!

Sometimes they try to convince you that they love you. But you're not a thing. Can he really love you? In most cases he is not in love, he's simply infatuated. It's easy to mistake infatuation for love. Infatuation is a big word to describe a foolish or all-consuming passion. If someone is infatuated it means he or she is a little carried away. He's all-in, going strong, and then just as quickly gets bored and is on to the next big idea.

> Infatuation is characterized by a lack of trust, lack of loyalty, and lack of commitment.

Guys get excited about being in a relationship. They may even go to extremes and be all-in—that is, ignoring friends and interests and pouring all of their attention into the new, exciting girlfriend. The problem is, a new and exciting infatuation only lasts so long. Guys start acting bored, and girls feel pressure to do things like going further physically so the relationship doesn't get stagnant or old.

If there is genuine care and affection, your relationship won't depend on getting physical. Want to put your relationship or next relationship to the test? Try a "thirty-day, no-touch" experiment. For one month, don't so much as hold hands or hug. Instead of developing the physical part of your relationship, you will be forced to develop the emotional side. In other words, you may get to know one

i'll mistake your infatuation for love.

2. They will make the thirty days and be bored with each other because the physical element was removed, showing the imbalance of emotional and physical connection.
3. They will make the thirty days and have a great connection because the infatuation with the physical had been replaced by conversation and creative activity.

The other test is the "family test." When a guy spends time with a girl's family, he sees her not as a thing, but as a daughter and sister. His interactions with her parents help him to be wise in how he treats someone so precious to them. It helps him know if what he is feeling is a passing infatuation and how to proceed in the relationship.

How would you do on these two tests?

. . . .

Try this in the next week:

1. If you are in a relationship with a girl, spend time with her family and get to know them.
2. If you begin to view a girl as a thing—something to be possessed—remind yourself of Who created her.
3. Instigate the "thirty-day, no-touch test" for the next thirty days, and repeat it at least twice a year after that.

don't mistake my infatuation for love.

continued

another even better, even faster. Besides, if it's just a passing infatuation, you're better off knowing that right away.

Guard your heart and take your relationships slowly. It may be that a guy loves the *idea of you*, but not necessarily you. A guy loves the idea of a girl on his arm, wearing his jersey, watching and waiting for him at his games. He loves the idea of physical affection and being desired. He wants a shot at being the protector and leader in a relationship. He's all-in and hyper-focused on the excitement of being in a relationship...for now. Let him protect and honor you and show you real affection or move along.

A relationship is not something to guess at. Pulling petals off of a flower to find out if he loves you just doesn't work. Take the "thirty-day, no-touch test." You don't want to mistake his infatuation for love.

. . . .

Try this in the next week:

1. Make a list of three attributes about yourself that you love the most. Does the guy in your life affirm those three things? Is he really excited about you...or just the idea of you?

2. Try to distinguish between something you've loved and something you've been infatuated with. Can you think of an example of each and recognize the difference?

Be strong and courageous. Do not be afraid; do not be discouraged, for the LORD your God will be with you wherever you go.

JOSHUA 1:9

Aim at heaven and you get earth thrown in. Aim at earth and you get neither.

C. S. LEWIS

SECTION 4

....

what gets girls/guys worked up

....

The tunnel of love is a lazy boat ride that winds its way through three minutes of uninterrupted silence and darkness. In a world of terrifying roller coasters and thrill rides, the tunnel of love is a timeless, romantic journey at carnivals and fairs. At least that's what she said.

Many girls secretly hope that he'll hold her hand and whisper sweet nothings into her ear as they drift down the tunnel of love. For three whole minutes she's not competing with any other girls, food, or sports for his attention, and she loves that! Moments like this get her emotions worked up.

Guys get worked up too, but for different reasons. Some may consider it a personal challenge to get something physical started and finished in three minutes flat. If he can't break down her barriers on a slow boat ride in a dark tunnel, he may never be able to. At least that's what he said.

The next few chapters concentrate on unpacking what gets guys and girls worked up (the good and the bad)... and why!

"I feel close when a guy tries to make me feel better when something is wrong. When he makes sure I know he's there even if I don't want to talk about it."

that's what she said

"When guys stop and ask for directions—I'm impressed."

"When they say 'I'm sorry' and don't give excuses, I respect that."

"I feel good when they listen to what I have to say and don't judge me."

"It makes me happy when they don't cross boundaries with what they say or do."

"I get worked up when girls whisper and giggle right in front of me."

that's what he said ◄ • • • •

"When they are genuinely interested in who I am and what I'm saying, I can tell there's respect."

"I respect a girl who is nice-ish to my friends even if she doesn't like them."

i need a little r-e-s-p-e-c-t

> i want you to treat me well—consistently.

> i crave your respect.

> # i want you to treat me well—consistently.

When teens are given the opportunity to ask questions about the opposite gender, some of the inquiries are humorous and others are telling. The classic questions from the guys are, "Why do girls go to the bathroom in groups?" and "Why do they take so long to get ready?" The girls ask things like, "Why do guys make everything a competition?" and "Why do they smell so bad sometimes?" All valid questions. I wish there was time to discuss all of them, but there isn't.

However, there is one that is too important to be ignored. Girls often ask "Why do guys treat me differently when they're around their friends?" With much agreement from other girls, they will share and compare evidence of the difference in treatment. There seems to be no problems when a guy is with just the girl. The two hang out at her parents' cabin. They laugh, joke, and catch major air while tubing. At night, around the campfire, they talk easily about how things are at home and where they want to go to college. At that moment, she feels connected to him and cared for by him.

> "I feel like you want a dog, not a boyfriend."
> A guy's response to a girl complaining that he doesn't greet her with excitement.

Scenario number two, however, is much different. It is usually set somewhere on school grounds. A guy is with his buddies, joking and shoving as they talk about the football game from the weekend before. She walks up to ask a simple question and with a quick glance at the guys, he acts annoyed with her question. She asks if anything is wrong and he gives her a short, cold "No." She tries to make eye contact with him, but it's too late, he's turned his back. She walks away confused—what happened to that guy from the cabin?

Girls understand the need to keep up a certain image. For them it often comes down to how they look, their grades, and their social status. They do, however, try to treat guys with care, attention, and respect no matter how much they have going on. So they get frustrat-

i crave your respect.

From playgrounds to prison yards, from Congress to the Congo, many a fight has started over a guy feeling disrespected. Universally, guys have a huge desire for respect. They are territorial. Their egos are sometimes fragile. And their pride can easily be hurt. Respect is key.

Guys live by a code among other guys—a code of respect. There are unspoken rules that honorable guys follow:

- Don't make a move on another guy's girlfriend.
- Don't disrespect another guy by disrespecting his girlfriend.
- Don't joke about another guy's mom.
- Don't pull any cheap shots on another guy.

The funny thing is, guys are okay fighting—as long as it is fair. They can punch and push and still go home as friends. Fighting fair is within the code.

When it comes to girls, guys really care a lot about having their respect. They want to be admired and trusted. They want to provide protection, leadership, and advice. Guys want you to appreciate them for their talents and skills, and recognize them for their accomplishments (ever notice how they keep trophies on display forever?).

> Studies show that men need and even want respect and affirmation from women far more than love.

Take a look at greeting cards next time you go shopping. Mother's Day cards are all about your love for mom. Father's Day cards are all about your respect and admiration for dad. The Bible tells us that a man must love his wife, and a woman must respect her husband (Ephesians 5:33). Guys are wired to need your respect (just like girls are wired to want a man's love).

How do you show him respect? If you ask him how to communicate your respect, he might say:

- Don't make fun of me, put me down, or call me stupid.
- Please don't laugh or giggle about me with other girls.
- Recognize and acknowledge my talents and accomplishments.

i want you to treat me well—consistently. continued

ed with the way the majority of guys seem to treat them two different ways, depending on the social setting. They hope for (and deserve) more.

Is it too much to hope for guys to consistently treat girls well? What would that look like? It could look like this:

- Making eye contact when she talks to you.
- Being happy to see her and showing that with a smile or calling her by name.
- Stepping away from the guys for a minute to say hi when she approaches.
- Calling when you say you're going to call.

If there are times when you need to be alone—like when you lose a wrestling match or are in the middle of Calculus homework—just gently let her know. If she has the confidence of knowing you care for her, she'll be happy to give you your space.

A lot of girls gauge the stability of their guy friend's/boyfriend's relationship by how he responds to her. The more consistently you treat her, the better it will be for her heart and for your relationship.

. . . .

Try this in the next week:

1. When you're with your guy friends and a girl approaches you, try stepping away, and paying attention to her before stepping back into the circle of guys. How does that feel?
2. Work on giving your girl friends eye contact. (It's actually something great to do with everyone!)
3. If a guy you're hanging out with treats a girl poorly when you're with him, call him on it.

i crave your respect. continued

- Ask for my help when you believe I can help.
- Don't cheat on me or flirt with other guys.
- When I try to be serious, please take me seriously.
- Watch me work and play, and tell me when I do a good job.

This whole love and respect thing can really blow up to create hurt feelings. Michael was out of town on his girlfriend's birthday, but he made a special point to buy her a thoughtful souvenir. His girlfriend didn't feel loved when her special day went by without a gift from Michael. She called Michael crying and told him he was thoughtless and selfish. Michael was crushed to hear that she lost respect for him, and in turn was defensive and short-tempered. It was a vicious circle that kept her from feeling loved and him from feeling respected.

Learning to speak girls' language of love and guys' language of respect is difficult because they're each so different. But isn't it good to know that God is behind this design? When you are in doubt about how to react to a guy, try giving him the respect the Bible says he needs.

. . . .

Try this in the next week:

1. Ask a guy for help with something (only if you truly need help and only if you truly believe he can help you). Give him positive feedback if he does a good job.
2. Tell a guy friend something that you admire about him. Be sure to be genuine.

Chapter 16

do you see what i see?

i'm insecure about how I look.

i'm a visual creature.

i'm insecure about how I look.

You see a girl walk into a room. You are actually observing carefully for once, so you notice she is what you would describe as "hot." She's tall, but not too tall. She is dressed like the models you see in the windows at the mall. (By the way, have you ever really looked at those models? Most don't have arms. Or heads. That's just weird.) Her face is beautiful—about twenty-three less zits than are on your face. Her body has everything in the right place with the right size. Her chest is big, her waist is small. Her hair is long on her head, but not on her legs. Her arms are toned, but you're certain you could still beat her in arm wrestling. Plus, she's walking through the room like she owns it. Wow.

> Girls can quickly tell you what they would change about themselves, but struggle to identify what they like about themselves.

Now, let me tell you what is most likely going on with this hot, not-going-to-beat-you-in-arm-wrestling girl. Hours before she walked into that room so confidently, she most likely stood in front of her mirror staring hopelessly at her reflection. Her jeans don't fit the way they are supposed to— her butt looks way too big. Someone certainly is going to notice that her boobs aren't as big as they really look—she's just wearing a bra with a bunch of padding. Even though she used a lot of make-up, she can still see her zits. Her arms look like twigs. Her hair is a disaster. Her last thought as she stepped into that room with you was probably something like, "I'll be amazed if people don't scream in horror and run when they see me."

Every teenage girl—and most adult women, to be honest—are insecure about how they look. It's understandable when you think about it. From the start of our day, we are met with images of the ideal woman. Magazines. TV. Billboards. Internet. Movies. Music videos. Clothing stores. We can't get away from what society seems to be telling us we should be. It stinks, and unfortunately, it matters way too much to us.

i'm a visual creature.

Guys are, for the most part, visually charged, sexual beings. Just like solar panels on a roof can generate enough power to heat an entire building, and just like wind turbines can generate enough power for a community, guys' eyes can provide enough food to feed their sex drives for days. They consume mental images and videos and convert them into sexual fuel. Their eyes are the gateway to their mind.

Marketing takes a visual form for guys because advertisers know it's effective. The most expensive television ads during the Super Bowl usually feature women in bikinis—in an effort to sell products (that have nothing to do with bathing suits) to guys.

If you want a guy to take you seriously and be more interested in you as a person than how you look or dress, think carefully about how you put yourself out there. Are you dressing and acting like the kind of girl who guys talk respectfully about or like the ones they drool over but would never bring home to Mom?

Campers in the wilderness are careful to store food in airtight containers. They go a step further and suspend the containers from ropes high in the trees. Knowing that bears are attracted to the scent of food, they go out of their way to keep the scent from the bears. If they're not careful, they will have unwanted, dangerous company while they sleep.

> Men gather 90 percent of what they need to know through what they see.

In the same respect, understanding that guys are visually stimulated, how can you avoid getting into dangerous territory? It's not that girls are responsible to overcompensate for guys' behavior. It's more like girls should avoid tempting guys (which usually results in exploiting themselves at the same time).

If a girl puts herself out there as nothing more than a pair of boobs, that's likely how a guy will see her. Some guys will party with a girl like that, but they won't build a real relationship based on physical traits alone. And they probably aren't the kind of guys you deserve.

i'm insecure about how i look. continued

All the blame can't be put on media, though. Most girls seem to struggle from insecurity all on their own. They look in the mirror and can't see what is obvious to others. They critique themselves constantly—nothing is ever good enough. They strive to be content with who and what they were created to be, but for most of them that's tough. Psalm 139 says that we were created inside our moms to be wonderful, unique, and of great value. Most of your girl friends and classmates want to believe it and live that truth, but most of the time, insecurity wins out.

So the next time you see a girl walk into a room looking like she has all the confidence in the world, don't believe it. She's most likely struggling. A kind word from you could make all the difference in the world.

· ·

Try this in the next week:

When you see a girl in your class, youth group, or neighborhood, say one of the following statements (but be sure you mean it):

1. "You look really nice today."
2. "I like your hair."
3. "I like hanging out with you."
4. "I think you're fun."
5. "You're a really cool friend."

i'm a visual creature. continued

It's fair to say that some girls like knowing the power they have over guys. They use their looks to get a guy's attention. They dress their bodies to keep guys interested. In some cases these girls send signals that guys read loud and clear—just because they like to see guys drool. They like the power of having a guy be like putty in their hands. The sad thing is, this strategy hurts everyone involved—the guy and the girl. Does knowing that guys are visually charged make you think twice about the way you relate to guys?

The Bible says that our bodies are not our own—when we treat our bodies well, we give God honor. Girls can honor God by respecting themselves in how they dress and present their bodies. Have you noticed that it genuinely feels better when a guy gazes into your eyes and not any lower? It feels better because it feels more respectful and it's more honoring to God. When the sexual element is decreased, a real relationship has a better chance to increase. And it makes guys feel better because they are honoring God too.

. . . .

Try this in the next week:

1. Ask yourself, "What message am I trying to send by wearing this outfit?"
2. What can you do to make sure you aren't intentionally or unintentionally setting yourself up to be seen as an object in a guy's eyes?
3. Write down one or two things about yourself that you want guys to take the time to see.
4. Ask yourself a tough question: When you use your body to get attention, in that situation are you a tool for God or a tool for the enemy?

Chapter 17

your power over me

> your words have so much power.

> your touch has so much power.

> ## your words have so much power.

Our brains are amazing organs! They're like crazy intense computers, constantly receiving and sending information. The memory seems to be limitless. I mean, just think of all the information that is stored in your brain. Your locker combination. A play out of the handbook. Lyrics to songs. Lines from your favorite movies. A-Rod's stats from his rookie year. It's all there—ready to be pulled up at any given moment.

One of the things that stick in our brains forever are words that have been spoken to us. Positive words. Negative words. Like MP3s, we can instantly pull those voices up in our minds and hear the messages all over again.

Girls remember words spoken about them like guys remember sports stats.

Because many girls struggle with comparing themselves to others and being insecure with how they look, they are more sensitive to words than guys. When girls talk about their elementary and middle school years, they can recount, word for word, things that were said about their appearance, intellect, clothing choices, and so much more. Those are words that will impact many of them for the rest of their lives (even with lots of prayer and counseling). Words can't be taken back. They stick around forever.

When I was in seventh grade and dominating the softball diamond, I hit four home runs in one game. I was so excited the next day at school when they announced that fact over the loud speaker. As I floated up the steps onto the school bus with pride that afternoon, I hoped someone would say something about my home runs. Nate, the goalie for the hockey team, was the first to bring it up. "Heather, I heard you hit four home runs. What did you do, put all your weight behind it?" Ouch. Those words stuck. Thanks, Nate. I had no idea I had weight issues—so glad you pointed it out.

When a girl likes you, the power of your words is intensified. Right or wrong, it's like she turns the volume of your voice up in her head—like you would crank your favorite song. She longs to be encouraged,

your touch has so much power.

Little boys can't keep their hands to themselves. They poke dogs in the face. They pull cats' tails. Their fingerprints adorn every glass surface in the house and car. Their crusty boogers line walls at just the height they can reach. Little boys push in line to be toward the front and fight in the backseat of cars with siblings. They are universally led into trouble by their hands.

Teenage guys are touchy too. They wrestle, prod, and push each other. They're grabby and rough. Some guys even give big bear hugs to one another!

We all know that guys are physical animals. They love full contact sports. They are usually bigger and stronger than girls and they love to use their muscles. Touch is a big deal.

And *your* touch is the perhaps the most powerful of all.

When Greg's girlfriend squeezed his upper thigh, his leg twitched and he was nearly paralyzed for a few moments. She probably had no idea how powerful her touch could be. She probably had no idea that she tripped off a launch sequence in his body. The littlest touch can quickly get a guy worked up.

As their blood leaves their brains to fulfill another function lower in the body, guys don't think quite as clearly and become vulnerable to your touch. Some girls are quite aware of the power they possess and try to use it to their advantage. They use their bodies—and his body—to get what they want. Maybe they want attention at that moment. Maybe they want to date him. Maybe they want his touch because they crave to be accepted. Whatever the motivation, it's a tragic situation because it ties the girl's worth to his physical reaction to her and exploits his vulnerability to touch.

While your other four senses (sight, hearing, smell, and taste) are located in specific parts of the body, your sense of touch can be experienced all over.

your words have so much power. continued

adored, and affirmed—and she looks for a lot of that in what you say to her. Your words have so much power. They can send her soaring or knock her down. Regardless, they will be stored in her brain for retrieval later.

What will you do with that power? Use it for good! Use it in a way that honors God. You can commit to thinking before you speak—understanding that once spoken, words can't be taken back. You can bite your tongue when sarcastic or hurtful words come to mind. With simple words, you can build up your friends and make a difference in their lives. Are you ready to use your voice for good?

. . . .

Try this in the next week:

1. Commit to be a positive voice in the minds of people around you.
2. Be thoughtful in the things you say to your girl friends.
3. Pray that God will help you keep quiet when your words could be hurtful.
4. Thank someone in your life who has been a positive voice in your head.

your touch has so much power. continued

In most cases, guys haven't thought about the power of touch. All they've figured out from what they've heard from big brothers and teammates is that touch feels good and they should get as much as they can. There are expectations out in the world—both said and unsaid—that a guy should be physical with girls or he's not living up to being a man. But that is not true.

Jon had an epiphany—a new discovery—when he thought deeper about the place for physical touch and closeness in his dating life. Jon realized that making out, something that used to feel like a right-of-passage, was just a nice word for foreplay. And foreplay sounded a lot like something that belongs in marriage, not dating. His relationship with his girlfriend really took off after the physical stuff slowed down. Their focus was back on each other, not each other's bodies. Unfortunately, it takes awhile for most guys to realize this. Until then, help them by making sure you both keep your hands to yourselves.

Touch is a big deal to guys. Your touch has the potential to help them lead well in relationships or it can sabotage the relationship and stunt true intimacy. If you want to build a strong, real relationship, be very careful with how you use touch. Your behavior can make all the difference.

. . . .

Try this in the next week:

1. Recall one example of physical touch that has hurt your ability to experience true intimacy with a guy. Have you had an epiphany like Jon's?
2. Think of two non-touch examples of how you can increase the emotional intimacy in your current relationship or next relationship.
3. Refrain from casually touching the guy in your life and see if it makes a difference in how he treats you.

Chapter 18

thinking of you

> i just want a few romantic gestures.

> i want a conquest more than a romance.

i just want a few romantic gestures.

Whether it's because we're hopeless romantics or just a little self-centered, girls want to be thought of often. But even better than being thought of is being *shown* that we're thought of often. When guys think of us and let us know, we feel valued. We feel remembered. To us, it means we're on your mind. It means romance! We like that.

One weekend, Esy went out of town to spend time with her grandparents. She was bummed to miss time with her boyfriend, but she loved her grandparents. Plus she had access to e-mail so she could still stay in touch with her boyfriend. Friday night, she sent an e-mail, letting him know how much she missed him and asked what he had done that night. She was excited to read his e-mail the next morning, but there wasn't one that morning, or that afternoon, or that night. She came home on Sunday so discouraged. How could he have not thought about her all weekend?! Esy found out from friends later that she was "all he talked about" when their group hung out and that he missed her terribly.

A gift thoughtfully chosen from the dollar section at Target could score you major points!

The truth is, guys, girls think about you a lot during the day. Way more than you think about them. That's okay, but when you *do* think about them, they want to know! A small gesture can mean big romance to girls. Some examples include:

- You eat with your family at her favorite restaurant and text her while you're there to let her know.
- You're meeting her at the theater and buy a bag of her favorite snack.
- You're at camp the week of her birthday, but arranged for your best friend to bring her a gift and balloons to her house on her big day.
- She loves lilacs (that's a kind of flower) so you pick some on your way to pick her up, giving them to her at the door.

i want a conquest more than a romance.

You may have grown up watching Disney movies that depict love and romance. You may have no deeper desire than to meet a prince charming who will sweep you off your feet someday. Brace yourself for some disturbing news: Most teenage guys aren't looking for a romance as much as a conquest.

Nine times out of ten guys will go as far physically as you let them. Sounds romantic, right? They are almost as interested in seeing what you'll let them do as they are in actually doing it. Whether we're talking about a seventh-grade guy who wants to try French kissing or a high school guy who wants to go much further, these are not the products of romance.

Nate went on a mission trip to Mexico with a group of students from all across the country. For one week their team taught kids at an orphanage, painted buildings, passed out shoes to kids with bare feet, and helped in any way they could.

If you asked Nate what the highlight of his trip was, he'd tell you it was kissing Britney. Nate was attracted to Britney the moment he met her that week. On the last night of the trip, they found their way to a hill that overlooked the city and Nate made his move—a big smooch on the lips.

And the next day they went home to their respective states and never spoke again.

Nate wasn't looking for a romance in Mexico—he was looking for an adventure. It was new, fresh, and exciting to have the attention and affection of a pretty girl. But not for a moment did he ever consider this as a long-term relationship. It was exciting and challenging to get a kiss in before time was up.

What do you think was going on in Britney's mind? Probably a lot more than Nate was ever thinking about. Nate's only intent was to fulfill an impulse and live up to a challenge. Do you think that one kiss meant the same thing to Britney?

> A firearm safety class consists of a minimum of twelve hours of classroom and field experience. No such training course exists on romanticism.

i just want a
few romantic gestures. continued

- You write a sweet message on a sticky note and place it on the next blank page when returning her notes from the class you missed.
- You grab a blanket before you head to the hockey game, because you know she always gets cold sitting on the metal benches.
- You text her during the day with a simple, "How's your day going?"
- You slide a note into her locker so she'll find it later.
- You save her a seat at youth group.
- You have the chance to see a certain movie, but chose another one because you want to wait to see the movie she likes with her.
- You are posting some random song lyrics on your Facebook page and take the time to write "Hi" on her wall.

Guys in our culture have it easier than ever! A simple text or wall post can build romance and her respect for you. Communicating is simple and convenient. You don't even have to talk most of the time! When you are thinking of her, put it to action—you *and* she will be glad you did!

. . . .

Try this in the next week:

1. When you see something that reminds you of her, text her and let her know.
2. Invest in some colorful sticky notes—then add color to her world!
3. The next time you're downloading something from iTunes, pay the extra ninety-nine cents to get her favorite song.

i want a conquest
more than a romance. continued

Most guys are like hunters. They want to explore the terrain, scope out their prey, and come home with something to show for it. Guys who fish undoubtedly have a story about the "big one that got away" because they long to have a trophy catch to prove their ability! Some guys who hunt and fish don't even keep what they catch—they just want to see if they can do it. It's all about the challenge.

Ben was like a hunter. He saw every girl as a new challenge. He was a womanizer. He would sweet-talk any girl he could. He had the gift of manipulation. So, often he got his way with girls. He didn't want to know them for who they really were. He wasn't interested in starting a long-term committed relationship. Ben wanted a conquest. And he wanted to see how far he could get with each girl. Every girl who said "yes" was a boost to his low self-esteem. He had a twisted way of thinking, really.

Beware of the Nates and Bens of the world. Not all guys are like that. Be careful that your longing for romance isn't masking the real intentions of a hunter like Ben. Look for a guy who wants to know you, not one who uses romance to manipulate you. Now that you know the truth, you can make decisions about your relationship that will keep it real.

. . . .

Try this in the next week:

1. Next time you're in the mood for romance, rent your favorite Disney princess movie with the girls—don't rely on teenage guys for your romance fix!
2. Write down one idea you have that will help you avoid becoming a guy's conquest when you date.
3. Stick to the "thirty-day, no-touch test" to make sure you are more than a conquest.

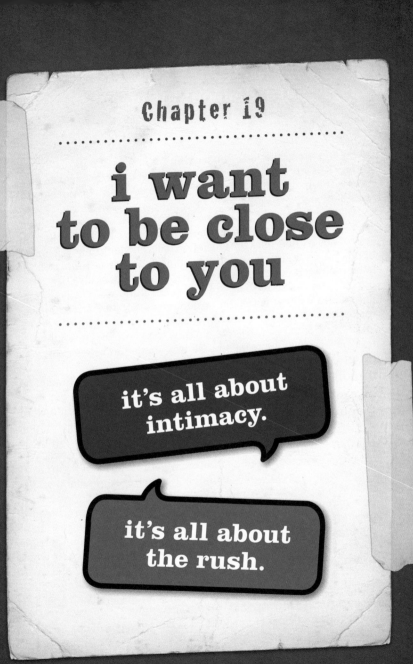

Chapter 19

i want to be close to you

it's all about intimacy.

it's all about the rush.

it's all about intimacy.

Guys aren't the only gender with hormones and sexual urges. Girls were created by the same God and given similar desires. The major difference is in what fuels the sexual desires of guys and girls.

Guys tend to be stimulated by the things you can see and touch. That's why car, motorcycle, and boat shows are such a hit with men. Thousands of guys flock to convention halls and fairgrounds to spend hours seeing and touching the machines. They love to inspect the latest shiny red Porsche and sit on the vintage Harley bike. The same principle translates to things of a sexual nature. When guys see an image of a woman with little or no clothes on, they are stimulated (pulse quickens, hormones surge, body responds sexually). In the same way, when a girl puts her hand on a guy's thigh or bicep, he responds. He was created to be excited by his senses of sight and touch.

> Men spell intimacy S-E-X and women spell it T-A-L-K.
> Gary Rosberg

Girls were created with a different kind of stimulation. Although we enjoy the sight of a good-looking guy, what fuels us is intimacy. It's kind of a big and loaded word, but intimacy is simply the closeness or familiarity girls feel because of shared experiences, words, or emotions. When guys say things that make us feel affirmed, connected, loved, or noticed, we are attracted to them.

I remember being at a church lock-in when I was in high school. Because we had nearly twelve hours to fill, we played four rounds of "sardines." If you have never had the privilege of playing sardines, you have not yet lived a full teenage life! With all the lights shut off in the whole church building (and lighted signs covered where possible), one person would hide and all others would try to find the hider. Once a "finder" would find the "hider" she would join in hiding in that same place, no matter how small of a place. This process would continue until everyone but the last finder was hiding—packed like sardines—in the same spot.

On this particular night, Jason was chosen as the hider. Because I

it's all about the rush.

Have you ever gulped a Slurpee or frozen drink too quickly and had "brain freeze" set in? It's a paralyzing, painful experience. Or belly-flopped into a swimming pool? How about back-flopped? (Otherwise known as the Nestea Plunge—look it up on YouTube.) A lot of guys stumble upon painful activities like these and quickly turn them into entertaining contests and challenges to tackle with friends. On purpose!

For years a popular television show has featured guys goofing off and hurting themselves on purpose. There's something about broken bones, blood, scars, and vomit that tugs at many guys' hearts. The gross and disgusting, the painful and scary, all contribute to "the rush" that gets guys worked up. Whether they're about to sky-dive from an airplane or eat a bowl of worms, the blood gets pumping and adrenaline takes over. An alarming number of guys love the rush of jumping off of a roof or skateboarding behind a car. They love to do what others are afraid to do.

> A stick in the yard becomes a magic wand in the hand of a girl and a sword in the hand of a boy.

God created guys' hearts to be adventurous. In general, they are explorers, warriors, and risk-takers, more so than girls. Guys want to be champions and victors. They value strength, and many covet scars as proof of their toughness. They are physical and love to feel. Watch teenage guys sometime and you'll see them punch each other in the arm just because and laugh!

Asking a girl out can be scary—and that can feel like a rush too. A guy might spend a lot of time thinking about what he'll say to ask her perfectly (although you'd never know it by the clumsy disaster that often comes out of his mouth). If she says yes, he feels like a warrior who just won the battle—his juices get flowing, and his ego gets puffed up, and it's all a big rush.

Where girls crave intimacy, too many guys crave the rush of physical adventure. Pushing physical limits with a girl gives them the same

it's all about intimacy. continued

had (and still do have) exceptional finder skills, I was the first to find him. For the next twenty minutes, we were smashed next to each other, talking and laughing in hushed tones. When the lights came back on, my intimacy level with Jason was at a record level. I don't remember being attracted to him before that night, but I sure was after that shared, quiet, fun-filled round of sardines! But what was eye-opening intimacy for me, was just a game to him. I was ready for the next level of relationship and he was ready for the next round of sardines!

Intimacy is huge to girls—that connection with a guy that makes her feel understood and appreciated. That closeness makes her feel special. Girls, more than likely, don't *want* to be sexual, but when they are stimulated by the presence of intimacy, they are more tempted to give in. That is how important your closeness is to girls.

That means that you have a huge responsibility to be genuine and sincere. Be honest. Be real. Be respectful. It is the manly thing to do!

. . . .

Try this in the next week:

Tom suggests the following (from one guy to another):
1. Take time to thank God for creating you to be a sexual being. It's a cool gift that will be a blessing when you are married!
2. Note how advertisers market to the different genders. Try to name specific words and images they use.
3. Be careful how you communicate with girls you are not interested in dating—they can easily perceive your words or actions as a desire for intimacy.
4. If your girlfriend is touching you in a way that sends your hormones raging, remind her of your commitment to long-term purity and how she can help you with that goal.

it's all about the rush. continued

kind of rush as doing a handstand while riding a bike. There's nothing romantic or special about it. It has nothing to do with love or care for you. The stream of consciousness in those kinds of guys' heads may sound something like this:

She looks hot tonight...I'm totally going to try to touch skin...she's never let me do that before...she French kisses so maybe she'll let me...I should at least try...I bet she'll totally let me...I'll probably wait until after we talk a bit... but then I'm going for it...I've gotta tell the guys...they'll be so jealous!

By the time this average Joe makes his big move, his body is running in overdrive. He craves the rush of going where he hasn't gone before. He loves what's dangerous, what's risky—even though he may know that getting physical outside of marriage is wrong. He wants to see if he can get away with it as much as he wants to actually do it. In short, a guy like this is not really thinking about you.

Finding the rush is fun on the paintball field but hurtful in a relationship. Don't let guys treat you like an extreme game or thrill ride to find their rush. Demand respect. Wait for the guy who will value you more than a risk. You're worth so much more!

. . . .

Try this in the next week:

1. Pause and inspect: are you mistaking physical attention from a guy for intimacy?
2. Be honest with yourself—are you playing games with a guy because you like to put him to the test? Physically, emotionally?
3. If the answer is yes, are you willing to make a change? If the answer is no, how do you stay on this safe path?

Therefore, I urge you, brothers and sisters, in view of God's mercy, to offer your bodies as a living sacrifice, holy and pleasing to God—this is your true and proper worship. Do not conform to the pattern of this world, but be transformed by the renewing of your mind. Then you will be able to test and approve what God's will is—his good, pleasing and perfect will.

ROMANS 12:1–2

In the faces of men and women I see God.

WALT WHITMAN

. . . .

what girls/guys think about sex

. . . .

Guys think about sex...a lot. And girls think about sex too, just not as much or in the same ways as guys.

Sex is God's beautiful, wonderful idea. God made sex for us to enjoy. But you need to know that the devil wants nothing more than to ruin your chances of experiencing sex the way God designed it. That's right—the devil delights in ruining your sex life!

Guys are sexually driven, yet many of them desire to do all they can to control that drive—out of honor to God and respect for women. But how should a girl react to a guy who doesn't? How does her behavior help or hinder their relationship? Does she even think about sex the same way he does?

When we delight ourselves in God, He gives us the desires of our hearts. These final chapters will help you understand where guys and girls are coming from when it comes to sex, and will challenge you to delight yourself in God's way of thinking about sex.

"I feel respected when guys can actually look at me as someone to indulge in a conversation with and not just a sex object."

"I like it when guys try to get to know you, they listen, and don't try things you're not ready for."

that's what she said

"When they keep their hands off me, I feel valued."

"I don't really care about where we go on a date, or what we do, because to me, conversation is key."

"Not all guys are out to just use girls. Some guys actually want a working relationship where love is wanted rather than sex."

that's what he said ◄ • • • •

"The perfect 'dream' date for me would be having a nice dinner somewhere kind of low key, but filled with great conversation and laughter. All that matters is that there's something to talk about. It doesn't matter where you go or what you do, but that you're just with someone that you care about having great conversation."

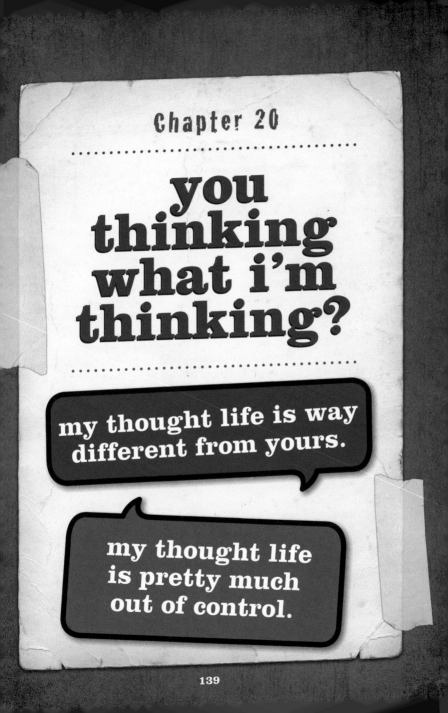

my thought life is way different from yours.

Maybe you've heard someone say, "Guys think about sex every seven seconds!" Wow. How is that even possible? How could a guy concentrate on something as simple as driving a car or following a math problem in class if he thinks about sex that much? Well, according to the The Kinsey Institute's FAQ, 54 percent of men think about sex every day or several times a day. That's quite different from once every seven seconds!

> Guys hope for a physical interaction. Girls hope for an emotional interaction.

Whether you think about sex every seven seconds or several times a day, girls think about sex a whole lot less than you do! It's not that they don't think about it at all, it's just not the primary focus in relationships for girls. Their sexual thoughts are more curious in nature. They wonder things like, "Who will it be with?" "Where will we be?" "What will he say to me?" "Will it hurt?" "Will I like it?"

Instead of thinking about sex often, girls think (and talk to each other) about feelings, hopes, dates, flowers, touch, and the future. Their thoughts usually don't match well with yours. When you're thinking one thing, she's thinking something altogether different. For example:

- If he thinks, *Wow, her butt looks hot!* She thinks, *Oh, he's noticing my new jeans!*
- If he asks, "Can I come over to your place?" She hears, *He wants to spend time with me!*
- If he says, "Come lay on my bed with me." She thinks, *Finally, he wants to cuddle and talk about feelings!*
- If he says, "I love you, baby." She thinks, *He wants to marry me!*

You can see how a relationship could develop tension. If the guy is thinking one thing and the girl is thinking another, both will end up feeling frustrated. It's good for couples to be honest with each other about boundaries and expectations. Communication is key.

We were created by God to be sexual beings. Because of this, it's

my thought life is pretty much out of control.

Sometimes guys think about sex the very moment they wake up in the morning and in the final moments before they fall asleep at night. They think about sex at school, while they watch TV, and while they work. When thoughts of sex pop into their minds, they often entertain the thoughts for a bit because they enjoy thinking about sex. They even dream about sex when they sleep.

Guys' bodies—producing ten times the testosterone girls produce—signal them to think about sex when they don't try to. By now you've heard of terms like nocturnal emissions and erections. In both cases, these events can occur without the guy even trying. In fact, sometimes guys wish these events wouldn't happen.

One guy was called to the front of the room and asked to lay on top of a table for a demonstration in health class. The teacher called on him because he was sleeping in his seat. When he heard his name he woke up but didn't want to stand up because he had an erection that would have been noticeable in his sweatpants. And he certainly didn't want to walk to the front of the class and lay on top of a table! This is not a problem girls ever have to think about.

> More than 50 percent of men think about sex every day or several times a day.

Guys have so much going on inside of them that sometimes it's difficult to *not* think about sex. Think of it another way. If your stomach growled, it would remind you to think about food. Guys' bodies remind them about sex at different times throughout the day. Do you know that, on average, a guy has an erection half the time he's asleep? So when he wakes up, there is a fifty-fifty chance he is thinking about sex.

Guys also choose to think about sex by their own free will. Every time their eyes wander from a girl's face down to her chest and butt they've made a choice. Every time they spend time on the Internet or watching TV in an inappropriate way they've made a choice. Every time they get physical with girls they've made a choice. And when

my thought life is way different from yours. continued

natural to have sexual thoughts or urges. So often, though, teenage guys struggle with an overload of sexual thoughts and desires because they are opening themselves to sexual messages through the Internet, music, movies, and/or television. God's Word challenges all of us (girls included!) to be cautious about what we allow into our minds and to think of things that are good, right, noble, true, and praiseworthy (Philippians 4:8). Be smart about what you watch and listen to. If you are, you'll experience a difference in how often and the way you think about sex.

. . . .

Try this in the next week:

1. Read Philippians 4:8 each day. Ask the Lord to help you to "think about such things."
2. Take an honest look at what you watch and listen to. Do the images and music push you toward a Philippians 4:8 kind of thought life? If not, remove these things from your life.
3. If you are in a serious dating relationship with a girl, initiate an honest conversation about the struggle guys have with thinking often about sexual things. Set boundaries that will protect both of you.

my thought life is
pretty much out of control. continued

they replay these things in their heads over and over again, they've made a choice.

Here's something interesting about guys that you might not know—many of them take mental pictures and videos that they file away for future viewing at their pleasure. That's right—some guys are like living, breathing digital cameras! You might break up with a guy only to have him continue to replay kissing or make-out sessions with you in his mind for years to come. Of course, there are guys who are different, who fight temptation and take control of their thought life. But either way, the temptation is there.

It is not your fault that guys' thought lives are out of control, but you can help. You help when you carry yourself with class. Dress with respect, date with respect, and carry yourself with respect—for youself and for your body. If you treat yourself with respect, you just might find guys will too. And that will help them get their minds off sex for awhile.

. . . .

Try this in the next week:

1. Ask yourself, "Do I ever put myself at unnecessary risk of being mentally recorded or photographed for future viewing?"
2. With the information that you learned in this chapter in mind, go through your closet and get rid of everything that you feel puts you at risk of being filed away as an object in a guy's mind.

Chapter 21

an appetite for sex

i know you want it.

give me a little and I want more.

i know you want it.

All a girl has to do is look around her and she sees that guys seem to want sex. Marketing is probably the most obvious giveaway! The purpose of advertisers is to sell product—and a lot of it! They wouldn't invest millions of dollars in a certain kind of marketing if they didn't believe it was effective. So, in order to be effective with guys, they load beer commercials with barely dressed, attractive women. Victoria Secret fills their display windows with curvaceous mannequins. They strategically schedule their runway ads during football games. Sexy sells to guys. Girls catch on.

> **The average teenage girl believes the lie that "everyone is doing it."**

If advertising isn't convincing enough, all a teenage girl needs to do is listen to the conversations of some of the guys around her. On any given school day, she'll hear comments like:

- How far did you get with her?
- She's hot!
- I'll tell you what I'd like to do to you....
- She's all that and a bag of chips! (Oh, wait...sorry, that's a comment from the 90s.)

So, what is a girl supposed to do with all this information? The following seem to be typical responses from many teenage girls:

- *All guys are scum.* With this philosophy, girls, especially girls of faith, will reject the idea of dating for a long time. They know guys want sex. They have committed to not have sex until they're married. So, they write off guys until at least college—assuming that all guys are the same.
- *If that's what guys want, I'll make them think they're going to get it.* With this angle, girls don't intend to have sex, but they give the impression they might. They tease by showing a lot of skin—low-cut shirts, short skirts and shorts, and low-riding, tight jeans. They'll touch you and flirt with you, using your sexual desire to fill a need they have for attention.

give me a little and I want more.

There's an old story about the battle between two huge, wild dogs. One dog lives in the dark and hides in the shadows. He whispers in your ear about wicked things and when you give in to his temptations, he accuses you and stabs your heart with guilt. His ways are easy and filled with pleasure, but his paths always lead to your doom.

The other dog is noble and lives in the light. He's under control, clean, and pure. He is humble, but make no mistake, he is a fierce warrior. He challenges you to follow difficult paths, but paths that will strengthen you and lead to joy. These two dogs fight continually within you.

Which dog to you think wins? *Whichever one you feed*.

> Every second 28,258 Internet users are viewing pornography.

There is a battle between good and evil that goes on inside every one of us. When it comes to guys, there is no greater tool used by the enemy—the devil himself—than sex. Sexual temptation is such a serious threat that we're not to turn the other cheek or stand strong in our position—we are to flee. In fact, sexual temptation is the *only* example in the Bible where God tells us to drop everything immediately and, with urgency, run for our lives. "Run from sexual sin! No other sin so clearly affects the body as this one does. For sexual immorality is a sin against your own body" (1 Corinthians 6:18 NLT). He knows that we can't face that type of temptation alone and win the battle.

When guys feed their sexual appetites—and when you feed their sexual appetites with provocative clothing, suggestive dancing, or immodest conversation—the temptation only grows stronger. It can bring life-changing consequences and lifelong patterns of destruction.

Pornography is feeding sexual appetites and hurting guys and girls in epidemic proportions. By the most conservative estimates, at least 25 percent of Internet usage is pornography related. Over 85

i know you want it. continued

- *I have no choice.* This perspective is probably the scariest of all! Girls with this idea give in to the sexual expectations and pressures with hardly a thought at all. They give their bodies (plus their hearts, minds, and souls—which are all linked together) to guys in order to be accepted. Sadly, they often find the acceptance to be short-lived. The guy usually moves on to other conquests and leaves them feeling rejected, guilty, and abandoned.

Gentlemen, here is the truth learned through years of working with teenage guys: guys are sexually driven, but many of them desire to try to control that drive—out of honor to God and respect for women. All men are not scum. All guys aren't out to just get a piece of a girl. But can you see how girls could think the opposite? Help change their perspective by talking and behaving with respect. Just because you have an appetite for it, doesn't mean you have to let it control you.

Try this in the next week:

1. When buddies at school or church start talking sexually about girls, be bold enough to stop the conversation.
2. Ask your youth leader to coordinate a time for all the guys in your youth group to have an honest conversation about our culture's sexual assumptions about guys and how you can combat those.
3. Ask the Lord to give you the courage and discipline to be a different kind of guy in the way you treat sex.

give me a little and I want more. continued

percent of guys in their teens and twenties visit pornographic web pages at least once each month. This addiction and obsession with sex hurts guys because it clouds their minds with evil thoughts and warped views of sex and relationships. It changes their hearts to crave impurity and darkness. It causes them to see girls as objects, creating unrealistic expectations for their future relationships.

Guys' sexual appetites are also fed by what is considered "normal teenage behavior." When guys and girls dance suggestively at school dances, each move is fuel for his sexual desire. When guys and girls make out, it's like pouring gasoline on a flame. His internal engine revs higher and higher with each degree of body heat raised. Many guys are fueled by hanging out at the beach, checking out girls in skimpy clothing, or browsing Facebook and MySpace photos. When he feeds that "dark dog," he is drawn away from the path of purity that God has for him.

The take-away from this is not to make guys out to look like monsters of some sort. It's to help you understand that temptation and porn can become a "hungry dog" in their lives that grows out of control. Now that you know, you can be careful not to be an appetizer.

. . . .

Try this in the next week:

1. Look through your Facebook or MySpace photos and, for your sake and his, remove images that could be used to "feed the monster."
2. If you're physically active with a guy, take a week off from touch, and see what happens. You may be surprised to see how physically out of control your relationship has become.

Chapter 22

what are you saying?

> i want you to keep it between us.

> everything we do will become public information.

i want you to keep it between us.

I have been inside a guys' locker room. Seriously, I have! Granted, no guys were in it, but I got a pretty good feel for what it's like. Unfortunately, even though no guys were present, my nostrils were still overwhelmed with the stench of sweaty socks, shoulder pads, and cleats. Wow. Fortunately, because guys weren't lining the benches, I didn't have to experience the stench of their crude, degrading, embellished accounts of physical encounters with girls.

I don't know what it is about locker rooms, lunch tables, cars, or the backseats of the bus that seem to encourage some guys to brag about their sexual experiences with girls, but I know we, as girls, don't like it. Girls pretty much universally believe that what is done and said between guys and girls should be kept there—between them. When you talk about physical experiences with other guys, it makes girls feel degraded, cheap, vulnerable, and used. If you really like a girl, I can't imagine those are ways you want her to feel.

. . . .
**Lying
is theft.**
. . . .

There are way too many stories of girls who have been devastated by guys who couldn't keep their mouths shut. Madison, for example, had only been dating Cole about two months, but she really liked him. Because she liked him and thought she could trust him, she kissed him. Madison liked how it made her feel and how it seemed to connect them, so she kissed him quite a bit. Even though she could tell Cole wanted more, she didn't go any further.

Every day at lunch, Cole and his high school buddies would sit at the same lunch table and talk about the same things—what they had done with the girls they were dating. Because Madison had drawn a healthy boundary in their physical relationship and most knew she wasn't "that kind of girl," he knew no one would believe it if he lied. So, instead, he started bragging about his sexual exploits with another girl (which were not true). Word got back around to Madison and she was shocked, humiliated, and heartbroken. Even though her reputation wasn't affected by his words, they were destructive to her heart. Imagine how that hurt could have been eliminated if Cole had

everything we do will become public information.

Most guys don't keep diaries. Most guys don't pour out their feeling to their best friends. They usually don't whisper. Guys don't place as high a value on keeping secrets as girls do. And guys like to kiss and tell!

Sometimes they kiss, or get physical with a girl, as much for the story to tell as the experience itself. Picture yourself as a guy who's never had a kiss. But all of your friends have, or at least they say they have. The longer you go without a story to share, the quicker suspicion grows among your friends that there's something wrong with you. See why they would want the experience? Guys face enormous pressure to tell of their sexual explorations.

Amazon.com
sells muzzles
for only $5.75!

I have a feeling that girls tend to minimize their sexual experience with guys when they share and guys tend to embellish or exaggerate theirs. Many guys also speak out of both sides of their mouths. They will tell you it's private, they will promise to keep it between the two of you, but in the end, it almost always gets out. Unfortunately, many guys are more concerned about their image than yours. And the stories that catapult their image to their worldly friends can hurt yours. It's really a terrible double-standard that too many guys buy into. So don't buy into guys that buy into that!

Sadly, when those guys talk about your physical beauty and your physical activity, they are focused almost entirely on what you *do* versus who you *are*. In previous chapters we've talked about how guys find their success in what they do, so they focus on actions. At times, this also causes them to value you for what you do more than for who you are.

Make sure you are spending time with a guy who likes to share all of life with you—walks, homework, church, friends, games, and even his pizza! Focus your activities on things that bring out who you are. If your relationship centers on what you do when you're alone, you're in trouble. Because in that arrangement you'll need to consis-

i want you to keep it between us. continued

just put a cork in it when he sat with his friends at the table.

Girls need to do some work in the "keep it between us" category as well. Although we don't tend to talk in large groups about what we do physically, we do tend to share just about everything else: What guys say. How guys look. What guys don't say. Girls read out loud the texts and notes you send. They evaluate nearly every word of your conversations. That's not fair to you. With the complexity of relationships, you don't need thirteen other girls knowing your secret conversations any more than you need to know theirs. If you both pay attention to the words you are saying and protect your relationship, it can grow into something even better.

. . . .

Try this in the next week:

1. If another guy says something like, "Hey, how far have you gotten with her?" look him straight in the eye and tell him that's between you and your girlfriend.

2. If you have friends that are girls who try to overload you with details of their relationships, let them know that you believe the guy would appreciate it if she kept it between them.

3. Ask the Lord to give you discernment in your sexual boundaries and in the way you talk about your girlfriend.

everything we do will become public information. continued

tently deliver or it will break down. If that's the case, your relationship is already in trouble. And he's likely sharing those stories of your "alone" time with everyone at the lunch table.

Don't kid yourself—whatever you do with a guy will most likely become public information. As long as you keep that mindset, you won't be surprised if/when it happens. In fact, if what you really do with a guy isn't juicy enough, some guys will add details to make it sound more exciting to his friends. It's the nature of teenage guys. Some good guys do the right thing and keep it quiet, but are you willing to take that chance?

Even if it doesn't become public information, do things that you wouldn't mind hearing about on a loud speaker. Don't risk your reputation, purity, or future. Spend time together with your boyfriend in groups, in public, or in "safe" areas. In *all* things honor God.

Try this in the next week:

1. Think about the latest sexual gossip you have heard about girls in your school or church. The way to make sure stories like that aren't told about you is by making sure nothing happens.
2. Pray for those who are the subject of the latest gossip.
3. If you're in a relationship, have a heart-to-heart with your boyfriend and let him know that you expect your relationship details to stay private. If he breaks your trust, you need to move on.

Chapter 23

....

setting boundaries

....

i can't always be the one to make us stop.

i don't make good decisions lying down.

i can't always be the one to make us stop.

Despite what you have heard or what you may believe about sex, here's the truth: Sex was created by God for the pleasure, intimacy, and enjoyment of couples who are married. It's true! When Adam and Eve were in the Garden of Eden, they were naked and felt no shame. After being united by God, they were told by Him, "Be fruitful and increase in number." Sex was invented by God to be a *fun* way for married people to "be fruitful." It's only because of sin that sex has the reputation and lack of boundaries it does today.

According to society, sex is for our pleasure. Unlike God's intention, sex is often used to gratify ourselves with little thought of how it affects the other person or our future. Many teenagers admit that they and their peers seek sexual experiences in order to:

- feel more mature
- satisfy their curiosity
- be accepted
- keep the guy/girlfriend
- express love
- have fun
- rebel against their parents

I get why those reasons would seem to make sense, but sex outside of marriage will fail to satisfy. Sex does not increase maturity. Sex does not guarantee acceptance. Sex does not keep your guy/girlfriend committed to you long-term. And sex without marriage is not biblical.

A five-minute conversation on sexual boundaries may save you months of fighting pressure.

Because God loves us and wants the best for us, He put some loving boundaries around the gift of sex. Hebrews 13:4 says, "Marriage should be honored by all, and the marriage bed kept pure." First Thessalonians 4:3–5 adds, "It is God's will that you should be sanctified: that you should avoid sexual immorality; that each of you should learn to control his own body in a way that is holy and honorable, not in passionate lust like the heathen, who do not know God." God wants us to honor His gift of sex by

i don't make good decisions lying down.

People on a health food kick usually try to avoid the ice cream stores and chocolate shops. Recovering alcoholics are more successful when they avoid taverns and pubs. There are many times when it's best to avoid the tempting situations that might put even the strongest will to the test. For guys, lying down with girls is about as tempting as it gets.

When it comes to your relationships with guys, the most challenging aspect is likely going to be setting physical limits and sticking to them. How do you know what is okay and what isn't? How do you tell a guy to stop? A lot of girls think they can let the guys make the decisions about how far is good and what boundaries are okay to cross.

> Guys need at least one accountability partner outside of their relationship.

Here's a not-so-well-kept secret about guys: they don't make good decisions lying down. More specifically, they struggle with physical boundaries when they're caught up in the passion of the moment (like kissing on the couch). That's because so much is going on in their bodies. Hormones are raging, and their decision-making abilities haven't quite caught up. When they are lying down next to you, they are more likely to forget about important things like boundaries, pledges, and where their hands are supposed to be.

Here are three tips for you to keep in mind when you are dealing with guys and boundaries:

- *Agree on physical boundaries ahead of time.*
  When you make decisions about boundaries ahead of time, you release the majority of the pressure because the decision is made. Be specific when you discuss your boundaries so he'll know how to show his affection and show you respect at the same time.
- *Boundaries can be overpowered by sex drive.*
  The closer you edge toward the limit of your boundaries, the more difficult it will be to stop. The more he gets worked up, the foggier his thinking becomes. The Bible tells young men to

i can't always be the one to make us stop. continued

enjoying it in a safe, committed, God-centered marriage. Until then, He asks us to control our bodies in a way that is honoring to Him.

In order for sexual purity to happen, girls and guys need to work together on a plan. It doesn't happen naturally and shouldn't only be the girl's responsibility. These steps can help:

- **Decide how far you want to go physically before you're married**. Choose a time when your hormones aren't raging (not when you are snuggled up with your girlfriend) and determine your personal boundaries. Remember, most Americans won't get married until after age twenty-five. If you only want to kiss until you marry, for instance, you should wait as long as possible before kissing. Stick to the boundaries you set.
- **Communicate boundaries with the person you are dating or about to date**. It's an awkward conversation for most teenagers, but it's essential. The other person deserves to know what they are in for.
- **Stay out of tempting situations**. Have your girlfriend over to your house only when your parents are home. Keep the lights and your clothes on. Don't lie down together.
- **Find someone to keep you accountable**. Choose a friend or older adult who can check in with you concerning your boundaries. Make sure it's someone who has similar goals and isn't afraid to get in your face.

Setting sexual boundaries and sticking to them is something you can do. It is not just the responsibility of girls. After all, you have to live with the decisions just as much as they do. Share the responsibility and to stick to the plan. Purity is worth it. God never said it would be easy, but He's given you everything you need to succeed and enjoy life!

. . . .

Try this in the next week:

1. If you are dating someone now, work through all four steps above.
2. If you are looking forward to dating, prayerfully work on step one.
3. If you have gone too far with a guy, ask God to forgive you and to help you set better, stronger boundaries in the future.

i don't make good decisions lying down. continued

"flee" from sexual temptation—to literally run for their lives. That's because God knows how He made guys, and He knows they will struggle with sexual temptation. Take away the struggle by not flirting with your boundaries.

- *Your commitment to boundaries is a huge help.*
  I'm a terrible dinner guest because I feed the family dog under the dining room table. The dog loves me in that moment, but the owners go crazy dealing with a dog that begs for food in the future. Do you see the connection? Stick to your boundaries with guys—no exceptions. If you cave in even once, you'll make it much harder for him to stick to the boundaries you originally agreed on.

Expecting him to remember and respect boundaries while you are lying down together is like expecting to put out a fire with gasoline. Setting boundaries in place and reminding him (and yourself) of them from time to time will help keep both of you in check.

. . . .

Try this in the next week:

1. If you are in a relationship, have a conversation about physical boundaries and agree on ground rules. Use specific language so you aren't trying to guess what the other means.
2. Think of one safeguard that will help you honor physical boundaries with guys (one idea may be to never lie down together).

Chapter 24

moving the boundaries

being physical will make you happy.

being physical will make me happy.

> ## being physical will make you happy.

A girl will do a lot for a guy she likes. There are teenage girls who commit to learning a new sport because the guys they like play it. Some have learned a foreign language. Others have taken up hobbies they used to dislike. I know girls who've cut their hair, chosen a school, and even altered their personalities to please a guy.

Some of the things a girl will do to make a guy happy are harmless and some are concerning. The most disturbing is when a girl will engage in sexual acts to please a guy. She is passing up a long-term joyful commitment for temporary pleasure and a perceived promise.

> God wants us to be holy, not necessarily happy.

Many girls have figured out that the average guy likes to be physical. They like to kiss, touch, and be aroused. I have talked with so many girls who battle with this—a guy is asking and pressuring her to go further than she wants to. She knows what she wants and how she feels, but she finds herself wanting to do it (whatever "it" is at that time in their relationship) to make him happy. The tricky part is, her decision seems to be the right one at the time...until the guy wants to move a step further, asking her to do more. His happiness, which she sacrificed so much for, only lasts a little while.

Girls find themselves in this situation because of their desire for relationships with guys. Girls who go too far (and usually end up hating themselves and the guy for it) do it for one of three warped reasons:

- "I want to get him!" Somehow in our society, the message has been sent to girls that they should use their bodies however they want...even to get a guy. Some girls will hook up with guys after knowing them for an hour at an amusement park. Some will give in to the "friends with benefits" type of idea in hopes that the guy will find out he really likes her. Don't be tempted by the offer. A relationship built on this kind of foundation will crumble quickly and take your self-esteem with it.
- "I want to keep him!" Once a girl starts dating a guy, the sexual

being physical will make me happy.

Guys think about sex a lot.

If they're not already thinking about sex, all it will take on your part is the slightest nudge in that direction and they will be back to thinking about it. The nudge might be intentional as you flirt, or it might be unintentional as you take off your sweater or bend over to pick up your purse. He'll be in the mood to be physical because it will feel good—and he thinks what feels good will make him happy.

Guys don't care about ambiance when it comes to being physical. The lights can be on or off—heck, the lights can be neon, florescent, or strobe and he'll be ready! You could be on a comfy couch or a wooden bench. You could walk along a moonlit beach or be crammed into the backseat of a car (in a sea of junk like gym bags, Gatorade bottles, and Doritos wrappers). You could be in a prom dress or have bad breath—he really won't care. Given the opportunity, most guys can get "in the mood" for physical affection in about one and a half seconds.

> The physical part of a relationship does not make it healthier or happier.

Guys are wired to desire a physical connection. In fact, without even realizing it, they might believe that the physical connection is key to discovering intimacy, trust, and closeness. They might believe that becoming more physical will deepen their relationships. That seems to be the message that bombards them daily. Most girls know that's not how it really works, but even they find themselves buying into it sometimes.

As a girl, you are more likely to desire an emotional connection with a guy. That doesn't mean you don't like the physical aspect—it just means it's not number one. But girls often find themselves compromising their boundaries, reasoning that it will make guys feel happy. Girls may believe that as long as he stays happy, he'll stay interested. Unfortunately, that is rarely true.

You've heard the old wives' tale about why kids shouldn't drink coffee because—say it with me—"It will stunt your growth." That's not really true—it's just something parents say to keep their kids from

being physical will make you happy.

continued

pressure increases. She is fully aware that there are other girls who will give a guy more. She really likes this guy! She doesn't want to lose him just because she's too strict with her sexual boundaries. Sometimes she moves her boundaries to keep him. If a girl is desperate enough to do anything to keep you, take a huge step back and talk about where your relationship is headed. This is where the "thirty-day, no-touch test" is needed most.

- "I want him back!" If a girl loses a guy, but still likes him, she may consider throwing her morals aside to get him back. This, too, is a slippery slope because you both are setting yourselves up for high sexual expectations the second time around in the relationship. Reuniting by lowering your standards is not a fair trade for giving up God-given purity.

When you know where a girl's weaknesses are, you can stand firm and protect the heart and reputation of that girl—just as she can be strong in areas where you have weaknesses. Understanding why girls cross boundaries will help you be the man you need to be. A real man respects the woman he likes. He is willing to draw a physical boundary to honor and protect her. Only immature, ignorant boys push and beg for more. A godly man will stick to the boundaries—even if she is willing to move them.

. . . .

Try this in the next week:

1. If you have ever pushed a girl to be more physical than she wanted to be, ask forgiveness of God and then her. This will lead you back to a healthy path.
2. Be mindful of the things you ask of your girlfriend. Be sure the things you ask of her are honoring her and the Lord.
3. Remember, one of your jobs as a warrior is to protect her sexual purity and reputation—do that well!

being physical will make me happy.

continued

drinking more caffeine. But what is true is that becoming physical too early in a relationship definitely stunts the emotional development of the relationship.

When Tyler and his girlfriend became sexually active, other parts of their relationship stopped growing. In fact, other parts of their relationship actually started regressing. Tyler's effort to plan creative dates waned. Instead of taking her to special parks and one-of-a-kind coffee houses, he really just wanted to make-out. Even their conversations became flat. They stopped growing closer emotionally—the truest sense of intimacy—because that just couldn't compete with the physical draw.

Tyler's girlfriend was devastated when they broke up. She had become more physical than she had ever planned to in hopes that it would make Tyler happy and bring them closer together. Instead, it stunted their growth as a couple and their relationship fizzled, leaving each with sexual baggage.

Rare is the guy who has a good handle on his sexual urges. It's all so new to him, and the messages the world is sending him are definitely not about how to control himself. The Bible says we should not have even a hint of sex in our lives outside of marriage. Let that idea—from the inventor of sex, God Himself—guide you next time you find yourself with a guy who's in the mood. Help change his focus from sex to other activities that make guys happy, like bowling, playing video games, eating, or watching movies with other friends. Finding things to share that don't involve intimacy may help you both remember where the boundaries are.

Try this in the next week:

1. What does it mean to you to not allow even a hint of sex outside of marriage in your life?
2. Remember that guys are supposed to be protectors. If you're with a guy who is not protecting your physical boundaries, cut him loose and tell him why.

Chapter 25

what the future holds

when we get physical,
i expect forever.

when we get physical,
i may not stop.

when we get physical, i expect forever.

Things that stick are intriguing to me. When I scribble something on a Post-it Note, all I have to do is slap it on a surface and it stays there. When I try to fit a huge sweatshirt into a little gift box for Christmas, I simply grab the tape and go to town. When I slide my cell phone into my backpack strap holder, the Velcro strip holds it in tight. Incredible.

Did you know that as male and female, we were made to stick? When a guy and a girl connect sexually, the intention is that they'll stick together for the rest of life. Check out Genesis 2:21–24:

So the Lord God caused the man to fall into a deep sleep; and while he was sleeping, he took one of the man's ribs and then closed up the place with flesh. Then the Lord God made a woman from the rib he had taken out of the man, and he brought her to the man.

The man said, "This is now bone of my bones and flesh of my flesh; she shall be called 'woman,' for she was taken out of man." That is why a man leaves his father and mother and is united to his wife, and they become one flesh.

They "become one flesh." They stick. Forever. Not only is that God's best plan for a couple, He also designed us to *want* to stick together. The intimacy of a sexual encounter is meant to bind a couple together. How does this affect you and your relationship with a girl? In several ways.

- When you choose to have a sexual interaction, you are Velcroing yourself together. The girl, especially, will feel intimately connected to you. Not just physically, but mentally, emotionally, and even spiritually.

- If after your sexual connection, you break up, it's like ripping that Velcro apart. It hurts deeply. Small parts of you, even though disconnected, are left with the other person—just like the fuzzy stuff that is always stuck to used Velcro.

- If either of you choose to date someone else and be sexual with them, you will adhere yourself again. You'll notice, however,

when we get physical, i may not stop.

Little boys often get in big trouble playing.

It starts off in the name of good fun. Tickling, pushing, running, and laughing. If you've ever babysat boys, you know what I'm talking about. They love to get worked up. But as they get more excited, their adrenaline and intensity rises. Pretty soon, what started off as playing turns into fighting, and play slaps turn into punches.

Big boys—teenage guys—have the same chemistry. What starts off as playful wrestling can quickly turn into fighting. As soon as an ego gets fractured, there's no going back. It's war.

> **Boundaries set in advance are vital to a healthy relationship.**

Most guys have a way of digging themselves into holes. Once they realize they've gone too far, they don't know how to retreat. Sometimes it's physical, like when play-fighting turns into real punching. But there are a few other situations where guys go beyond the point of no return and find themselves in trouble, like:

- Kevin and his girlfriend get into an argument and each say hurtful things to the other. As the argument gets more and more heated, Kevin has a harder time backing down or seeing the situation from her perspective. His competitive nature sends his focus to "winning" the argument rather than understanding.

- Ben and his girlfriend become sexually active but later regret their decisions. They set new physical boundaries but continually find themselves crossing over the new boundaries and falling into old habits. Their relationship is marked by broken promises, regrets, and strife. And they don't know how to fix it.

Generally speaking, guys don't know when to stop. It could be a maturity issue, a rebellion thing, an ego issue, or a lack of discernment—but it's likely a combination of all four. Some guys can get so far down a path they may not know how to retreat. Did you

when we get physical, i expect forever.
continued

that the connection isn't as sticky. The Velcro has lost some of its strength because it was torn away during the other break-up.

Sierra and her boyfriend, Sam, had sex three months into their dating relationship. She experienced some guilt the day after, but that guilt was quickly replaced by the need to "keep him." She texted more. She touched more. She demanded more. It wasn't because she had lost it mentally, but because she had experienced that intimate connection, and it changed everything.

Velcro was invented in 1941 by Swiss Georges de Mestral.

Guys, it's important for you to understand that once a girl experiences sticking with you, she'll do all she can to stay attached. In fact, many girls will become even more possessive, aggressive, and intense once you've become sexual because they don't want to lose the connection. They are expecting forever. If you are not committed to forever, stay away from sticky situations!

Try this in the next week:

1. Thank God for His divine plan for couples to stick together.
2. Ask a close, trusted advisor or mentor who is married to explain how being sexual after marriage changed his relationship with his wife.
3. Re-think your sexual boundaries. Are they strong enough to keep you and your girlfriend safe from sticking?

when we get physical, i may not stop.

continued

catch that? They literally may not *know how,* and they need someone to show them.

Have you ever noticed that the best athletes have good coaches? Guys typically respond really well to coaches even when coaches scream or swear. In fact, many guys like to be screamed at by their coaches. There's something inside of them that seems to think, *"If I listen to Coach, I'll be better."*

Unfortunately, most guys don't have mentors speaking truth into their lives, helping them grow and mature, nearly as often as they have athletic coaches on the sidelines. In the absence of a mentoring voice, guys are left to learn on their own—or worse, from each other!

Jack was lucky enough to have a mentor when he was involved in a serious relationship with a girl. When the teenage couple struggled to stay within their sexual boundaries, Jack's mentor encouraged him to take a break from the relationship altogether. Later the couple got back together with a fresh start, new perspective, and stronger accountability. But Jack needed the break and a mentor's help to figure that out.

It is important to realize that guys are in the early stages of developing their ability to lead and protect. There is a warrior inside that is fierce, but not yet completely under control. Once they've gone too far, that warrior may not know how to retreat. Don't be afraid to take a huge step back and take a break. You never know what the future holds.

· ·

Try this in the next week:

1. Whether you're in a relationship now or would like to be in one in the future, write down your boundaries for physical touch and closeness. (Bonus points if you share what you write with a mentor or trusted adult!)

2. If you have a boyfriend, ask yourself, *"Have we crossed any boundaries or gone too far down any roads?"* If your answer is yes, remember that he may not know how to fix the situation, and it may be wise to take a break and talk to a mentor.

my commitment—guys

Girls seem like a mystery to many, but you've done the work of studying girls, and the skies are beginning to clear! What will you do with the information you have learned?

Tom and I hope you will grow to understand where girls are coming from and celebrate your differences. If you do, you will have unlimited opportunities to enrich your relationships, guard your hearts, protect your purity, and honor God.

twenty-five truths about girls

Check each truth you've come to understand and respect about girls. Remember, each girl is unique, and all of these may not apply to the girls in your life but are meant as general guidelines. If you are unclear on any of these truths, reread that chapter and/or talk to someone you trust like a youth pastor, parent, or counselor.

- ☐ Girls will always want to spend *more* time with you.
- ☐ Girls want to feel safe and protected.
- ☐ Girls want you to read their minds and respond accordingly.
- ☐ Girls struggle with comparing themselves to others.
- ☐ Girls may try to fix you.
- ☐ Girls are dramatic.
- ☐ Girls are hopeless romantics!
- ☐ Girls often use their bodies to get attention from guys.
- ☐ Girls think of relationships as long-term.
- ☐ Girls talk a lot and may be confused when you don't do the same.
- ☐ Girls can be mean...especially to each other.
- ☐ Girls like physical strength, but are attracted to inner strength.
- ☐ Girls accumulate emotional baggage as they move through relationships.
- ☐ Girls may mistakenly interpret your infatuation as intimacy.

174

my commitment—girls

While guys generally are not as complicated as girls, learning how to understand them is still tricky. Now that you've done the work of studying guys, what will you do with the information you have learned?

Heather and I hope you will grow to understand where guys are coming from and celebrate your differences. If you do, you will have unlimited opportunities to enrich your relationships, guard your hearts, protect your purity, and honor God.

twenty-five truths about guys

Check each truth you've come to understand and respect about guys. Remember, each guy is unique, and all of these may not apply to the guys in your life but are meant as general guidelines. If you are unclear on any of these truths, reread that chapter and/or talk to someone you trust like a youth pastor, parent, or counselor.

☐ Guys would sometimes rather play video games than spend time with you.

☐ Guys want to be a hero.

☐ Guys can't figure out why I'm upset—I'll just need to tell them.

☐ Guys may not notice my new hairdo, shoes, or nail polish.

☐ Guys' brains are a few years behind their bodies.

☐ Guys are impulsive.

☐ Guys are not thinking about their future—they can't even spell marriage!

☐ Guys give me attention for the wrong reasons and that means trouble.

☐ Guys are not usually thinking about protecting purity.

☐ Guys are just learning how to talk to girls and can be insensitive and hurtful.

my commitment—guys

- ☐ Girls want guys to treat them well no matter who is around.
- ☐ Girls struggle with feeling confident in how they look.
- ☐ Your words carry a lot of power.
- ☐ Girls want a few romantic gestures from you.
- ☐ Girls are stimulated by words, emotions, and shared experiences.
- ☐ Girls' thought lives are way different than yours.
- ☐ Girls are aware of how much guys focus on physical things.
- ☐ Girls want everything you do together to stay private.
- ☐ I shouldn't expect the girl to be the one to make us stop.
- ☐ Girls mistakenly believe that being physical with you will make you happy.
- ☐ Girls believe that getting physical means a forever relationship.

Personal commitment: I commit to honor God by celebrating the differences between girls and guys. I will use the knowledge I gained to respect and encourage the girls and women in my life.

_____   _____
Your signature   Date

my commitment—girls

continued

- ☐ Guys can be selfish.
- ☐ Guys are insecure about what you think of them.
- ☐ Guys are not attracted to girls with baggage when they are ready to be serious.
- ☐ Guys may allow their infatuation to be interpreted as love.
- ☐ Guys crave your respect.
- ☐ Guys are visual creatures.
- ☐ Your touch has a lot of power.
- ☐ Guys want a conquest more than a romance.
- ☐ Guys are all about the rush.
- ☐ Guys' thought lives are pretty out of control.
- ☐ Guys' appetite for physical things grows stronger when fed.
- ☐ Guys have a tendency to make private things public information.
- ☐ I shouldn't expect guys to make good decisions laying down.
- ☐ Guys mistakenly believe being physical with you will make them happy.
- ☐ Guys may not know how to stop once you get physical.

Personal commitment: I commit to honor God by celebrating the differences between guys and girls. I will use the knowledge I gained to respect and encourage the guys and men in my life.

_____   _____
Your signature   Date

Other books by...

Heather Flies
I Want to Talk with My Teen about Girl Stuff
Help! I'm a Woman in Youth Ministry
Great Talk Outlines 2

Tom Richards
iBelieve
iChoose

About the Authors

TOM RICHARDS is the program director of TreeHouse, an outreach ministry in the Twin Cities for at-risk teens. His passion is mentoring and developing the next generation of Christian leaders.

HEATHER FLIES has been a Junior High Pastor in Eden Prairie, Minnesota, since 1998. She spends a great deal of time as a youth communicator, speaking at junior and senior high schools throughout the state.

Also from Summerside Press™...

iBelieve and iChoose: Devotions for Real Life
by Tom Richards

The time between being dependent on parents and gaining their own independence is filled with questions and discovery for students. *iBelieve* and *iChoose: Devotions for Real Life* help teens and twenty-somethings identify what it is they believe and how to make choices based on those beliefs. Filled with daily stories about real people, Tom Richards shares his personal observations from years of working with students. The discussion questions may be used for self reflection or to share with friends in a small group.

iBelieve
Give them the tools to figure out exactly what they believe about God, prayer, friendship, heaven, hell, and the temptations they face.
144 Pages/$12.99
ISBN 978-1-935416-72-2

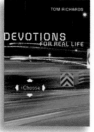

iChoose
Help them stand up for what they believe about faith, peer pressure, purity, eternity, and doing the right thing.
144 Pages/$12.99
ISBN 978-1-935416-73-9

For more information on these books and other Summerside Press titles, visit www.summersidepress.com. Now available at amazon.com, barnesandnoble.com, and christianbooks.com.